## ALL THE

Colin Swash started ~~writing~~ ... ever since he can rem... professional footballer. Now thirty, he has filled the time waiting for the big break by writing books and comedy scripts. Major works include *Jesus Phlegm*, a quite unpublishable first novel, *The Box*, a slightly better (but still unpublished) children's book, and scores of silly sketches for Radio 4's *Week Ending*. He is also co-editor of a forthcoming book of collected political wit and vitriol.

# COLIN SWASH

# *All the Fun of*
# AFFAIRS

Robinson

**ILLUSTRATED BY PETER ROBINSON**

A PAN ORIGINAL
**PAN BOOKS**
London, Sydney and Auckland

First of all, many thanks to Catherine Hurley and Judith Hannam of Pan Books for their cheerful efficiency and calm during the publication of this book. And thanks to Alan Maryon Davis for the introduction.

I would also like to thank the staff of the British Library and all libraries in the London Borough of Greenwich. Thanks too to my mum, for digging up some intriguing and otherwise undiscovered titbits.

Above all, thanks and much love – for support, putting up with me and everything else – to Karen.

First published by Pan Books Ltd,
Cavaye Place, London SW10 9PG

1 3 5 7 9 8 6 4 2

© Colin Swash 1991

Illustrations © Peter Robinson 1991

ISBN 0 330 31362 2

Photoset by Parker Typesetting Service, Leicester
Printed and bound in Great Britain by
Clays Ltd, St Ives plc

# CONTENTS

# CONTENTS

# CHAPTER ONE

# AT FIRST SIGHT

*First impressions,
favourable and not so favourable*

**"** **Who ever loved, that loved not at first
sight?**

CHRISTOPHER MARLOWE

Yoko Ono didn't even know who John Lennon was when they first met. She was busy setting up an exhibition of avant-garde art when Lennon strolled into the gallery for a look around. It was 1966 and the Beatles were already world famous, but Yoko was, in her own words, 'such an artistic snob', that she had no interest in their music or how they looked. However, she felt an immediate attraction to Lennon. 'He seemed so sensitive and imaginative ... The first thing that crossed my mind was that I wouldn't mind having an affair with a man like that.' Eighteen months after their first meeting, while John was still married to Cynthia, he and Yoko went to his personal recording studio and made electronic music together.

Not every couple hit it off as well as John and Yoko did. At the other end of the scale lie (in separate beds) King George IV and Caroline of Brunswick, who were committed to marry before they'd even met. It was repulsion at first sight. On seeing his future queen – short, fat and in dire need of a bath – George turned away in horror and ordered a large brandy. Caroline was no more impressed with her future husband. 'Is he always like that?' she asked an attendant at the court. 'I find him very fat and nothing like as handsome as his portraits.' They were married for twenty-six years, twenty-five of which they spent apart.

> **Love is the delightful interval between meeting a beautiful girl and discovering that she looks like a haddock.**
>
> JOHN BARRYMORE

Henry VIII would have sympathized with Caroline. He found the flesh and blood Anne of Cleves infinitely less desirable than the portrait of her painted by Holbein. The marriage had already been arranged and Henry's hopes had been raised by other reports of her beauty besides Holbein's portrait. After her voyage from Calais, the original plan was for Henry to meet her at Blackheath, but he was so excited at the prospect of meeting this fair goddess that he travelled on, incognito, to Rochester. He had come laden with presents to surprise her with, but in the end he simply had them sent on to her the next morning. Although tempted to sneak off as soon as he saw 'the Flanders mare', Henry introduced himself and they dined together that night. The wedding had been scheduled to take place the next day, but Henry postponed it for a couple of days while he tried to find a way out. Unable to come up with immediate grounds for her execution, he married her. The annulment followed a few months later.

Edward VII had better luck with Lillie Langtry three hundred years later. A sketch of her beautiful face had been mass-produced on cards which sold to the public for a penny each; when Edward saw one, he was determined to find out if she was as lovely in the flesh. A mutual friend dutifully arranged a dinner party. Mr Langtry was also invited, but he was no more than a spectator at the inception of one of British royalty's most celebrated affairs.

Nowadays, thanks to modern technology, physical attraction can be felt from afar without running the risk of being misled by a dodgy painter. But of course there can be other complications. Michael Caine first set eyes on his Indian-born wife Shakira in a television advert for coffee. Seeing her in what the advert assured him was a Brazilian paradise, Caine resolved to fly to South America to find her. Twenty-four hours later he was hot on her trail . . . but still in London. An actor friend had saved him the fare to Rio by giving him Shakira's London phone number. When they met, Caine found the real Shakira even more beautiful than the one 'advertised'. After their marriage, Shakira acted in just one film with him, *The Man Who Would Be King*, in which she got married to Caine's co-star Sean Connery. Her only line was 'Yes'.

The first time Ian Botham saw his wife-to-be Kathy, she was wearing hot-pants and long white boots – well, it *was* the seventies! Botham pointed her out to a friend with: 'She's a bit of all right.' He and Kathy did not actually meet until later, on a rainy day at Leicester's Grace Road cricket ground. Sitting with friends in the clubhouse, Kathy asked the stranger nearby if he had seen any cricket before the rain. Ian Botham replied that he had been playing. After that shaky opening, their romance blossomed. The last word, however, should go to Kathy's mum, who commented after first meeting him: 'What a nice quiet young man.'

'A bit of all right' was also the poetic expression that leapt from the lips of Peter Sellers when he saw a photograph of Britt Ekland in the newspaper. There and then he knew he had to meet her, which proved uncommonly simple, as it so happened they were both staying in the same hotel, the Dorchester. On their first date, they dined on champagne and caviare and then, presumably Sellers' idea of a treat, they went to see a Pink Panther movie, starring Peter Sellers as Inspector Clouseau.

But for Peter Sellers, Spike Milligan would never have met his first wife, June Marlowe. Although Spike was over thirty, he was still quite shy in female company; Sellers only persuaded him to join a party at a nightclub by agreeing to introduce Spike as a foreigner who spoke practically no English at all. And so, the first time the future Mrs Milligan met her husband, he was an Italian named Jules. 'Jules'' broken English caused plenty of laughter, though after a while some members of the party suggested he was really a bit thick. June leapt to his defence – just because Jules didn't speak English didn't make him stupid; he was a very nice person. At this Spike finally cracked up, and revealed his true identity. Two years later they married.

> **Many a man has fallen in love with a woman by a light so dim he would not have chosen a suit by it.**
>
> MAURICE CHEVALIER

> **The trouble with some women is that they get all excited about nothing – and then marry him.**
>
> CHER

The Duke of Wellington experienced a different sort of let-down when he met Kitty Pakenham for the first time in twelve years. As a young man he had twice had proposals of marriage rejected by Kitty's family, due to his 'unsuitability'. (It has even been suggested that these rejections were what spurred him on to his successful military career). He served in Flanders and India, but the pair kept in touch through a go-between, preserving their romantic pictures of each other and assuming neither to have changed. By the time of his third proposal, Wellington was a suitable catch by any family's standards. However, when he saw her again after their twelve-year separation, he turned to his brother, who was going to conduct the wedding service, and whispered, 'She's grown ugly, by Jove.' Unfortunately for both of them, they had also grown apart in personality. They went ahead with the wedding and were married for twenty-five years, but not happily; during the six years of the Peninsular War, Wellington didn't even bother to take any home leave. Nothing could match the ideal that both had held in their hearts during their twelve-year separation.

Charles Dickens would have been better off with memories of Maria Beadnell as a young mistress, than to arrange a secret meeting with her over twenty years after they had spilt up. The revival of their relationship started in a friendly correspondence by post. In one letter, Dickens asked her if she had noticed herself in the character of Dora in *David Copperfield*, 'a faithful reflection of the passion I had for you'. Before their meeting, Maria warned him that she had grown fat and ugly, but Dickens refused to believe it. When they finally met again, he realized she had been telling the truth. But far worse, her enchanting laughter had become an irritating giggle, and chatter that had once been infectiously energetic was now simply loud, dull and never-ending. Just as she had been the inspiration for Dora in *David Copperfield*, she was soon to be less flatteringly portrayed as Flora in *Little Dorrit*: 'Flora, whom he had left a lily, had become a peony; but that was not much. Flora, who had seemed enchanting in all she said and thought, was diffuse and silly. That was much. Flora, who had been spoiled and artless long ago, was determined to be spoiled and artless now. That was a fatal blow.'

Charles II was far from complimentary about the appearance of Catherine of Braganza, his queen-to-be, but appreciated that looks weren't everything. He couldn't be in Portsmouth when Catherine landed after a rough voyage from Portugal as one of his mistresses was heavily pregnant and he was reluctant to leave her. When he finally did see Catherine, she was not at her best, suffering from a cough and fever brought on by the luxuries of seventeenth-century sea travel. 'They have brought me a bat instead of a woman,' Charles informed a friend; nevertheless, he expressed himself 'confident our two humours will agree very well together'.

Charles III-to-be was impressed on his first meeting with Margaret Trudeau, wife of Canada's then-Prime Minister in the seventies, if Mrs Trudeau's word is to be trusted. Apparently he took a sly peek down the front of her blouse and told her she was 'pretty enough to be an actress'.

Some may care to argue whether or not Barbra Streisand is 'pretty enough to be an actress', but there is no doubting her talent in performance. Elliot Gould was already booked as the leading male in the Broadway musical *I Can Get It For You Wholesale* when a girl called Barbra Streisand came to audition for the bit-part of Miss Marmelstein, a fifty-year-old spinster. He was so knocked out that he phoned her that very evening, said three little words ('you were great') and then hung up. A year later they were married.

> **He's great-looking, but he's no Einstein.**
> BARBRA STREISAND (on Ryan O'Neal)

Ukelele man George Formby didn't go down too well with his future wife, Beryl, back in the early 1920s. The first time she ever saw him, he was playing live on stage and, as she later recalled, 'If I'd had any rotten tomatoes on me, I'd have thrown them at him.'

Nat King Cole's first view of Maria Ellington came when he was backstage watching her sing. 'Who's that?' he whispered to a friend. Taking in her name, he nodded approvingly: 'If

she looks as good from the front as she does behind ...'
Presumably she did. Their affair caused the break-up of his
first marriage and resulted in his second.

Neil Kinnock and Glenys Parry were both students at
Cardiff University when politics brought them together. Her
first words to him will not go down as the most romantic in
history: 'Are you the man from the Socialist Society?' Still,
Neil fell straight away for the girl who had once been Miss
National Savings, finding her 'not only lovely to look at but
also delightful to talk to'. At the Saturday night ball, he was
keen to dance with her, but was suffering a bit from a rugger
injury picked up that afternoon. The injury, together with the
few beers that he had knocked back for medicinal purposes,
led to a spectacular collapse on the dance floor. Marking the
start of a beautiful friendship, Glenys walked him home.

Margaret Thatcher had to put on a more dignified performance the night she met Denis, as it was at a Conservative
Association meeting for her adoption as the Conservative
candidate for Dartford. As ever, she had a tiring schedule to
follow, and needed to take the late train to Colchester in order
to be on time for work the next morning. When Denis entered
her life, it may not have been love at first sight, but she was
certainly delighted to meet someone willing to drive her to
Liverpool Street station. As for Denis, can it have been purely
out of party loyalty that he offered a lift to the striking blonde
in blue?

Cleopatra, Queen of Egypt, made an immediate impact in
her first encounters with the two great men in her life, Julius
Caesar and Mark Antony. In Act II of *Antony and Cleopatra*,
Shakespeare tells of her arrival at Tarsus, where Antony was
waiting to greet her. The purple sails of her golden barge were

'so perfumed, that the winds were love-sick with them . . .
For her own person, it beggared all description.' The way
Shakespeare tells it, Antony was the only person who didn't
rush to the shore to witness the spectacle. But in the end he
succumbed; although her invitation had been for supper, it
was mainly Antony's eyes that did the feasting: 'Other women
cloy the appetites they feed, but she makes hungry where
most she satisfies.'

> **Fat men make the best lovers. History is
> full of examples. Consider Cleopatra's
> choice of Caesar; he was no lightweight,
> remember. And it wasn't just hair that
> attracted Delilah to Samson, it was his
> remarkable girth.**
>
> PETER USTINOV

Cleopatra's appearance before Julius Caesar some fifteen
years earlier was equally spectacular. Caesar wanted to negoti-
ate a peace between Cleopatra and Ptolemy XIII, who were
brother and sister, husband and wife, and at war! If Ptolemy's
troops had known of Cleopatra's whereabouts and her plans
to visit Caesar, she would have been assassinated. She therefore had her servant carry a long rolled-up carpet into Caesar's
palace. Assuring Caesar that he would like what he saw, the
servant unrolled the carpet before him. But it was not the
pattern that caught Caesar's eye – at the centre of the roll was
Cleopatra! It says much for the lady's style that as she fell out
of the carpet, Caesar fell for her.

> **Royal wench!
> She made great Caesar lay his sword to bed
> He ploughed her, and she cropp'd.**
>
> *Antony and Cleopatra*

> **A woman can be big and still sexy. It depends how she feels.**
>
> ELIZABETH TAYLOR

The film *Cleopatra* was 'surely the most bizarre piece of entertainment ever to be perpetrated' according to the actress who played her, Elizabeth Taylor. She was reading by a swimming pool at a Sunday morning party in California when her Antony, Richard Burton, made his first appearance in her life. Burton recalled the moment when she took her glasses off and looked his way: 'She was so extraordinarily beautiful that I nearly laughed out loud.' Playing it cool, he carried on socializing, although he was constantly aware of her presence. When one anecdote he told went down particularly well with those around him, he turned, smiling, in her direction, only to find she was deep in conversation with someone else. Asked later what her first impression of Burton was, she replied that he seemed 'rather full of himself . . . I seem to remember that he never stopped talking and that I had given him the cold fish eye.'

> **I don't like females all dressed up — Eve in her original state is my ideal: natural, undecorated, modest without puritanism.**
>
> SEAN CONNERY

> **When you've got the personality you don't need the nudity.**
>
> MAE WEST

'I see him before me as he entered the house. A long thin figure, quick straight legs, light, sure movements. He seemed so obviously simple. Yet he arrested my attention. There was

Unity Mitford _was equally impressed with a certain Adolf Hitler, whom she first saw and heard speaking at the Nuremberg Rallies in 1933. 'From that moment,' she said, 'I knew there was no one else in the world I would rather meet.' Despite rumours that they had an affair, Unity and Adolf were, most probably, just good friends. All the same, for Hitler she might more fittingly have employed Lady Caroline Lamb's description of Lord Byron after *their* first meeting: 'Mad, bad and dangerous to know.'

66
**Love is a dream, wholly subjective.
People fall in love with the most
extraordinary people.**

NANCY MITFORD

Affairs don't always get off to a flying start. Mick Jagger hardly swept a seventeen-year-old Marianne Faithfull off her feet when he approached her at a party in the 1960s, introduced himself and spilt his champagne down her shirt. Unimpressed by his apology and his unsubtle attempts to mop her breasts with his bare hands, she walked off. As she left, she declared him the spottiest young man she had ever met. Soon they were lovers.

Benazir Bhutto's mother and aunt had both been scheming for years to set her up with a husband, but she was always too busy with politics to take any interest. So when at a party her aunt introduced her to a man named Asif, it never clicked that this was the latest eligible bachelor that Mum and Auntie Manna had been raving about. Benazir and Asif got talking, but very soon were arguing. Her aunt, who had been keeping a watchful eye over the pair, subtly moved in and led Asif away to meet another guest. All Ms Bhutto felt at that moment was relief that the man had gone. A year later, their wedding in Karachi was celebrated all over Pakistan.

> **It is difficult enough making friends with your own sex, let alone deciding to spend your life with someone of the opposite sex. It is not easy to be interested — and marriage means to be interested — in someone else all the time.**
> KATHARINE HEPBURN

Two great Hollywood romances also blossomed from unpromising beginnings. Spencer Tracy was too devout a Catholic ever to divorce his first wife, so he and Katharine Hepburn never appeared together in public as a couple during their twenty-six-year-long affair. It was Hepburn who nursed him through his illnesses and, in his final battle against death, helped him complete his last film *Guess Who's Coming to Dinner* to his satisfaction. They had first met to discuss making a movie; after their opening exchange, it was a wonder they made the film, let alone spent the next quarter of a century together. Hepburn was five feet seven in her stockinged feet, but her built up shoes added another four inches to her height. Looking down at Tracy, she commented, 'I'm afraid I'm a little tall for you.' Tracy, who felt her handshake would have been more suited to a hardened businessman, replied with a thin smile, 'Don't worry, I'll soon cut you down to size.'

Lauren Bacall was nineteen when she appeared in the film *To Have and Have Not*, playing opposite the man who was to become her husband, forty-four-year-old Humphrey Bogart. Bogart was already a famous film star but – before they met, at least – he was not exactly Miss Bacall's ideal leading man. When, after her first screen test, the director Howard Hawks told her he wanted to put her in a film with Cary Grant or Humphrey Bogart, Bacall's first thought was: 'Cary Grant – terrific! Humphrey Bogart – yucch!'

# CHAPTER TWO

# THE ART OF SEDUCTION

## Leading men and leading ladies, leading on and led astray

> " **Give me some music — music, moody food of us that trade in love . . .**
> CLEOPATRA, *Antony and Cleopatra*

Frank Sinatra is said to have treated his dates to a medley of his greatest hits as a means of seduction. Peter Sellers clearly thought if it was good enough for Frankie it was good enough for him. The hit comedy LP *Songs for Swingin' Sellers* owed its title to the Sinatra record *Songs for Swingin' Lovers*, but Sellers was wise enough to appreciate that his chances of success were far greater when he wooed his ladies to the sound of Sinatra. Besides the marked difference in mood and vocal perform-ance, any romantic atmosphere would most certainly have been wrecked by the sleeve of Sellers' record, which featured a hanged man 'swingin'' from a tree.

Placido Domingo is another singer to have made the most of his vocal talents to win a woman's heart. In his case, though, the problem was not so much wooing Marta Ornelas, his wife-to-be, as convincing her *mother* that he was the right man. Placido's years of global fame and fortune were still ahead of him, but the fine quality of his tenor voice rang round the neighbourhood as he treated Mrs Ornelas to a birthday serenade, accompanied by a group of buskers especially hired for the occasion. To all appearances, Placido was singing to his young sweetheart Marta, but he was sly enough to slip in plenty of songs from the repertoire of her mum's favourite Mexican singer. Events took a worrying turn when some unappreciative neighbours complained about the noise and called the police. However when the boys in brown turned up, they couldn't understand what the fuss was about. 'You're getting a beautiful performance,' the neighbours were told, 'free, by a member of the National Opera.' And so, with the police's blessing, Domingo continued his recital.

Q: When it came to live performances, what did Elvis Presley and Franz Liszt have in common?
A: *An eye for the ladies.*

Liszt, the Hungarian composer and pianist whose love life Ken Russell so lavishly brought to the silver screen, would often fix his eyes on a lady in the audience and gaze at her while he played, making her feel as if he was playing for her and her alone. The poet Heinrich Heine once wrote: 'Women become almost intoxicated whenever Liszt plays to them.' James Huneker, an American critic, put it another way, saying that he only had to look at the chairs after Liszt had been playing to know where the ladies had been sitting.

## LISZT LIVE IN LAS VEGAS

It never happened of course – Liszt dazzled the world with his showmanship a century too early for that – although some Bhuddist music lovers may claim he did play there, reincarnated in the form of Elvis Presley. There were certainly echoes of Liszt at Vegas in 1971, as Elvis crooned 'I Can't Help Falling In Love With You' and gazed directly into the eyes of a stunning eighteen-year-old blonde. At Presley's request, the 'beautiful piece of woman' in Row B was invited backstage. So began a very close, if very brief, relationship. 'He talked to me about God and politics,' the girl later reported – a risky combination of chat-up topics, which Elvis's many impersonators would be wise to keep out of their own post-act repertoire.

If Elvis, with his 'God and politics' line, stands at one end of the rock'n roll chat-up scale, the other end is fittingly occupied by the Rolling Stones. According to their former manager, Mike Gruber, the late evening conversation between a Stone and a hopeful groupie rarely stretched beyond the words: 'You – come with me.'

$S$ome things are better left unsaid. When Marlon Brando appeared in Charlie Chaplin's film *The Countess from Hong Kong*, he did not exactly sweep his leading lady, Sophia Loren, off her feet. Rehearsing one love scene, Brando gazed intently into her eyes, and then studied her nose. His next line – 'You have black hair in your nostrils' – was not in the script.

> **Sex appeal is fifty per cent what you've got and fifty per cent what people think you've got.**
>
> SOPHIA LOREN

$C$o-starring with Diane Keaton in the film *Reds*, Warren Beatty experienced little difficulty slipping into the role of

John Reed, the American author of *Ten Days that Shook the World*. Although his book is about the Russian Revolution rather than a wild week and a half spent making the earth move, Reed kept sex as high on his list of hobbies as Beatty does, and once talked a girl into bed with the line: 'Aren't you PAGAN enough?'

'Would you like to have dinner with an ageing movie star?' This modest one-liner scored a remarkably high success rate for the ageing movie star in question, but it must also have been a help to be called Cary Grant. In fact, Mr Grant was so modest that he would usually get one of his aides to approach the lady and make the proposition for him. On acceptance, the lady was whisked off to Grant's Los Angeles home, with its spectacular view of mile upon mile of unspoilt beach, for a discreet dinner for two. Whatever happened after dinner Grant managed on his own behalf, without further assistance.

**❝**

**Under twenty-one women are protected by law; over sixty-five they're protected by nature; anything in between's fair game.**

CARY GRANT

When Omar Sharif met Barbra Streisand for the first time, he kissed her on the hand and told her that she was the woman he had most wanted to meet in the entire world. Call it romantic charm, call it shameless crawling, it got him the male lead opposite Streisand in *Funny Girl*.

> **Never let a kiss fool you and never let a fool kiss you.**
>
> BETTY GRABLE

One of Bernard Shaw's many lovers was the striking Florence Farr, the first actress to play the role of Louka in Shaw's *Arms and the Man*. According to Shaw, her looks, manner and intelligence meant that every one of her male friends fell in love with her. She was so used to this, Shaw says, that she lost patience with those who obviously wanted to kiss her but couldn't bring themselves to make the final advance. 'Let's get it over,' she would say, grabbing the reticent Romeo and offering her lips to his. With the kiss out of the way, she would then calmly resume the conversation.

> **Don't get me wrong, I think fucking is a great sport. It's all the fucking talk you have to listen to from the man before . . .**
>
> AVA GARDNER

The wait before the first kiss does not always have to be agony. One exponent of sex with a smile was Richard Burton, who, according to fellow actor Warren Mitchell, 'laughed them into bed'. Certainly Elizabeth Taylor must have smiled when Burton approached her on the set of *Cleopatra* in 1962 and asked 'Has anyone told you what a pretty girl you are?' She was widely regarded as the most beautiful woman in the world.

Charlie Chaplin made a fortune out of his sense of humour, but it's debatable how much use he made of it in the bedroom. Posing starkers in front of a bedroom mirror and saying

'Don't you think I look like Peter Pan?' would be enough to raise a giggle from most lovers, if it weren't for the worrying thought that the man could be speaking in deadly earnest. Still, it can't have put off Joan Barry, a young Hollywood starlet, as she filed a paternity suit against him in 1944. Despite being described by Joan's lawyers as 'a master mechanic in the art of seduction', Chaplin was saved by blood tests that showed he was not the father of Joan's child.

Chaplin the mechanic was not always in the driver's seat. Peggy Hopkins Joyce, an alimony millionairess courtesy of five ex-husbands, came to Hollywood in 1922 with high hopes that it would live up to its non-stop party and scandal reputation. Over dinner for two with the great comedian, the conversation took an unexpected turn when Peggy eyed him over her glass and enquired if it was true what all the girls said – that he was 'hung like a horse'. There is no record of Peter Pan's answer, though it may explain why Charlie the Tramp's trousers are always so baggy.

'Let's go to bed – now!' *If the direct one-liner has anything going for it, it must be the element of surprise. Not that it's guaranteed to work . . .*

Shirley Conran, author of the racy bestseller *Lace*, was once propositioned while her head was in a gas oven. She was not trying to kill herself, just working out why the pilot light wasn't on. A friend she had known for years offered to help and looked in for himself. His head within kissing distance of hers, he blurted out the above suggestion. Shirley couldn't understand it. What had got into him? She was the Queen of Sex, he replied; at which Her Highness simply withdrew from the oven and shook her head in disbelief.

> **I do not go out of my way meeting girls;
> they have to meet me. It's the girl's job
> to introduce herself to a man.**
>
> MOHAMMED ALI

King Ludwig I of Bavaria was a more willing victim of surprise tactics when a shapely twenty-seven-year-old named Lola Montez burst into his private chamber, her garments in some disarray after the guard's attempts to stop her. Rather than rearrange her clothes, she decided she'd look better without them and so, picking up a pair of scissors from a nearby table, she cut through her bodice, from cleavage down to navel. Ludwig looked at Lola open-mouthed. A fine pair they must have made, for five days later, Ludwig was referring to her as 'my best friend'.

Actress Theresa Russell finally won the affections of Nick Roeg, the British film director, by means that Lola Montez would have been proud of. After flying across the Atlantic, she strolled into his office, wearing a mackintosh – with nothing underneath. She is now a respectably married sex siren and mother of two.

Robinson

One of the world's great composers of romantic opera, Giacomo Puccini, found plenty of time for real-life unromantic sex. He once described himself as 'a hunter of wildfowl, women and good libretti'. However, as his fame grew, more and more women came hunting for *him*. One morning, when staying at a hotel in Vienna, he received an intriguing phone call from a husky-voiced young lady demanding to see him immediately. Puccini granted her an interview and greeted her in his pyjamas. The girl was certainly very attractive, but Puccini's heart must have sunk to his slippers at the sight of a small boy holding her hand; even worse, in his other hand was a violin case. Had he been conned into giving a private audience to yet another so-called 'prodigy'? Happily, no. The girl quickly explained that her brother was on his way to a music lesson and would pick her up when he'd finished. The relieved Puccini retired to his bedroom to smarten himself up a little; when he returned to the other room, the girl was wearing nothing but a smile. In recounting that tale to a friend, the gallant Puccini commented, 'I felt too sorry for the lunatic to send her away.'

> **I kissed my first woman and smoked my first cigarette on the same day; I have never had time for tobacco since.**
>
> ARTURO TOSCANINI

'He pursued with no discrimination the married and the unmarried, the noble and the lowly . . .' Those words, applicable to many of history's Casanovas, were used to describe King Edward IV by a visitor to his court named Dominic Mancini. 'However,' Mancini added, 'he took none by force. He overcame all by money and promises and, having conquered them, he dismissed them.' Edward preferred older women (though, in an emergency, a young one would always do) and he only came unstuck when a widow named Lady

Elizabeth Woodville refused to succumb. 'My liege,' she said, 'I know I am not good enough to be your queen , but I am far too good to become your mistress.' Thus tempted, Edward eventually proposed marriage. Immediately after the service they went to bed and 'tarried for four hours'.

Well into his sixties, George II didn't want to waste any time with pleasantries when, at an evening function, he saw the Duchess of Kingston dressed in a costume that consisted of little more than a body stocking and a cleverly placed garland of flowers. Nostrils flaring, George sidled up to her and breathed into her ear an earnest request to put his hand on her breast. The Duchess gave him a sly look and suggested she guide his hand to an even softer place. As George stood there drooling, she took his hand and placed it on the top of his head.

> **If you wish women to love you, be original; I know a man who used to wear felt boots summer and winter, and women fell in love with him.**
>
> ANTON CHEKHOV

The Greek god Zeus appreciated the allure of an eye-catching costume. A shower of gold, a snow-white bull and a rain cloud were just some of the guises he adopted when visiting earth for a fling with a mortal. His most famous assignation was with a girl called Leda, on whom he pounced dressed up as a swan. W. B. Yeats described the scene in his poem, 'Leda and the Swan':

> How can those terrified vague fingers push
> The feathered glory from her loosening thighs?
> And how can body, laid in that white rush,
> But feel the strange heart beating where it lies?

How indeed, but what on earth did Leda tell her mother?

**Of all forms of caution, caution in love is perhaps most fatal to true happiness.**
BERTRAND RUSSELL

Bertrand Russell, one of history's randier philosophers, had radical views on education and even started up his own experimental school, Beacon Hill, with his wife Dora. The guiding principle by which staff were expected to conduct themselves was that of free love. By some strange coincidence, most of the teachers that the headmaster deemed worthy of a post in his school were young and female.

Sarah Bernhardt's bedroom had one unusual item of furniture – a silk-lined coffin, in which, it was said, she brought many a man to life.

**There's no substitute for moonlight and kissing.**
BARBARA CARTLAND

Potiphar's wife, whose attempts to seduce young Joseph are documented in the book of Genesis (and set to music in the Rice – Lloyd Webber musical *Joseph and the Amazing Technicolour Dreamcoat*), was taking a terrible risk, since the ancient penalty 'for seducing an innocent youth' was to have your nose cut off. Perhaps it was out of gratitude to be living in more enlightened times that Burton's boss Ralph Halpern liked to have his nose stroked by the 'innocent youth' Fiona Wright.

## NICE WORK IF YOU CAN GET IT

Rasputin, the Russian fireball widely known as the 'mad monk' was, according to his biographer Alexander de Jong, neither mad nor a monk. What *is* beyond dispute is that he

drove women mad . . . with desire. He started out with the noblest of intentions, though his methods were unorthodox to say the least, helping women in their battle against temptation by going to bed with them, kissing them and caressing them. Some girls he kissed and kissed and wouldn't let go of until they were so disgusted with kissing that they'd never fall foul of any passing stranger's charms. He would take baths with them and have them wash his private parts, which he kept under control to show he was beyond sin. However, somewhere in the course of providing this service, he was led astray. Perhaps it was the demands of the job, but after a while he began to take advantage of his alleged connections with the Almighty. One widow with whom he slept was a certain Madame Berlatskaya, who gave herself entirely to him or, as she put it, 'entirely to God'. In her diary she wrote that, the morning after, Rasputin told her how well she had purified herself, but then at night he again 'put her to the test'. Her conclusion was that she must be terribly impure to require such constant testing. Rasputin, in a break from their lovemaking, agreed: he had never come across such a tricky case.

# CHAPTER THREE

# WORDS OF LOVE

*Tender, tempestuous or trite —
love letters, and a touch of poetry*

Starting a love letter is never as straightforward as putting 'Dear Sir or Madam' – as the letters of both Bernard Shaw and Richard Burton testify. Here's Burton writing in 1983 to his last wife, Sally . . .

Dear Sally,
Or dearest Sally or most beloved Sally or undo-without-able Sally or lovely Sally especially with a minimum of clothes on, or clever Sally or sexy Sally . . .

66 **The ideal love affair is one conducted by post.**

GEORGE BERNARD SHAW

Bernard Shaw and actress Ellen Terry wrote to each other for fourteen years before they finally dared meet face to face, but their letters amounted to much more than mutual fan mail. Shaw started one letter: 'Ellen, Ellen, Ellen, Ellen, Ellen, Ellen, Ellen, Ellen, Ellen, Eleanor, Ellenest, . . .' For the lover, the name of a loved one can have a magic all of its own.

**66 At the touch of love everyone becomes a poet.**

PLATO

The love poems of Karl Marx do not figure prominently in the history of romantic verse, but his earnest outpourings were enough to touch the heart of Jenny, his wife-to-be.

> See! I could a thousand volumes fill,
> Writing only 'Jenny' in each line,
> Still they would a world of thought conceal . . .
> Truly, I would write it down as a refrain,
> For the coming centuries to see –
> *Love is Jenny, Jenny is love's name.*

While 'the coming centuries' pay more attention to *Das Kapital* and the *Communist Manifesto*, the remains of Jenny Marx lie in Highgate Cemetery beside those of the father of twentieth-century socialism, better known to Jenny as her 'dark little savage', 'Moor' or 'little wild boar'.

'Porchizia' (piglet) and 'Topizia' (little mouse) were just two of the pet names Giacomo Puccini had for his wife, Elvira. 'You will see what little orgies we will have,' he wrote to her, anticipating their imminent reunion. 'The evenings are the worst, and the poor little bed without my Topizia.'

> **Sensual pleasure without union of the souls is bestial and will continue to be so. No trace of noble emotion is left, only remorse.**
>
> LUDWIG VAN BEETHOVEN

Orgies were not Beethoven's idea of a good time. His was a more spiritual notion of love. The following is one of three letters written in his own hand, which were found amongst his possessions after his death. None of them had been posted.

Good morning on                                          7 July
Even when I am in bed my thoughts rush to you, my immortal beloved, now and then joyfully, then again sadly, waiting to know whether Fate will hear our prayers . . . Be calm — love me — today — yesterday — what tearful longing for you — for you — you — my life — my all — all good wishes to you — Oh, do continue to love me — never misjudge your lover's most faithful heart.
ever yours
ever mine
ever ours      L

The identity of his 'immortal beloved' remains a mystery to this day.

66
**Beethoven is about trying to get on with your wife. It is a reconciliation of opposites.**

COLIN DAVIS (conductor)

In contrast to Beethoven's intensity and suffering, Frédéric Chopin seemed less interested in the relationship between himself and Delphine 'Fidelina' Potocka, than the one between creativity and the male orgasm.

Fidelina, my one and only beloved:
   I will bore you once again with my thoughts on the subject of inspiration and creativity, but as you will perceive these thoughts are directly connected with you . . .
   To me inspiration and creativity come only when I have abstained from a woman for a longish period. When, with

passion, I have emptied my fluid into a woman until I am pumped dry then inspiration shuns me and ideas won't crawl into my head. Consider how strange and wonderful it is that the same forces which go to fertilize a woman and create a human being should go to create a work of art! Yet a man wastes this life-giving precious fluid for a moment of ecstasy . . .

What about Mozart? I don't know, but I think his wife became ordinary food for him, his love and passion cooled, and he therefore was able to compose a great deal.

. . . Who knows what ballades, polonaises, perhaps an entire concerto, have been for ever engulfed in your little D-flat major. I cannot reckon what might have been, since I have not composed anything for ever so long, immersed as I was in you and in love. Works which could have come to life, drowned in your sweetest little D-flat major, so that you are filled with music and pregnant with my compositions!

He rambles on for another couple of pages before finally signing off. And then (to prove his fidelity?) . . .

PS I have just finished a Prelude.

**❝ I'll never play the piano again . . .**
WOODY ALLEN
(after making love to Diane Keaton in *Annie Hall*)

'What about Mozart?' asks Chopin. It may have been envy rather than reason that led him to attribute Mozart's prodigious output to his wife becoming 'ordinary food' to him. Mozart's letters below were written after more than seven years of marriage and show no sign of the Seven Year Itch.

Berlin, 19 May 1789
Dearest most beloved wife of my heart!

... Oh, how glad I shall be to be with you again, my darling! But the first thing I shall do is to take you by your front curls; for how on earth could you think, or even imagine, that I had forgotten you? For even supposing such a thing you will get on the very first night a thorough spanking on your dear little kissable bottom; and this you can count on ...

Four days after the 'spanking' letter he's writing again:

Dearest, most beloved, most precious little wife!

... On June 1st I intend to sleep in Prague, and on the 4th – the 4th – with my darling little wife. Arrange your dear sweet nest very prettily, for my little fellow deserves it indeed. He has really behaved himself very well and is only longing to possess your sweetest *****. Just picture to yourself that rascal; as I write he climbs on to the table and looks at me questioningly. But the rogue is simply ***** and now the knave burns only more fiercely and can hardly be restrained ...

I kiss you millions of times and am ever your most faithful husband

W. A. Mozart.

Before he became Prime Minister, Benjamin Disraeli had several romantic novels published, and he made the most of his literary skills when writing to his future wife, Mary. In comparison to Mozart, though, he is miserly with his kisses ...

'I pass my nights and days in scenes of strange and fascinating rapture. Till I embrace you I shall not know what calmness is. I write this to beg you to have your hand *ungloved* when you arrive, so that you may stand by me, and I may hold and clasp and feel your soft delicious hand as I help your mother out of the carriage ... A thousand and a thousand kisses. More, more, come, come, come.'

The important thing when writing letters like that is to make sure they end up in the right hands. Marlon Brando Sr was proud of his young son's acting success, but sharing the same Christian name did cause a few complications. One morning, getting to the post before his son, he innocently opened a letter addressed to 'Marlon Brando', from an eager young lady who obviously did not have the older man in her sights. With a sigh for what might have been, Dad refolded the letter and scribbled across the envelope: 'Sorry, opened by mistake'. Due to the personal nature of the contents, Marlon Jr blew his top and insisted that, in order to avert future confusion, his father change his name. Marlon Sr's response was a firm No. Why should *he* change? After all, he'd had the name first!

In 1960, Joan Collins was passionately in love with Warren Beatty. Three times she broke off from filming in Rome and flew to New York just to spend a few hours with him. The romance came to an end when Beatty fell for Natalie Wood, his leading lady in the film *Splendour in the Grass*. Even worse for Joan, Beatty entertained the film's cast during a lunchtime break by reading one of her love letters out loud to them.

Before his more famous relationship with Wallis Simpson, Edward VIII, then Prince of Wales, had a long affair with a woman named Freda Dudley Ward. The first night they met they danced until 3 a.m. Aware that she was married, Edward sent a message to 'Mrs Dudley Ward' the very next morning, telling her he would be round for tea at five unless he received a message warning him off. Unfortunately for him, the lovely Freda was living under the same roof as her mother-in-law, who, since she was also a 'Mrs Dudley Ward', opened the letter herself. So excited was the older woman at the thought of the Prince of Wales coming to see her, that she asked Freda to go out for the afternoon. Edward must have suffered a mild heart attack when the clock struck five and his beaming hostess opened the door, but he survived their cosy tea for two and went on to enjoy an affair with the younger Mrs Dudley Ward for sixteen years, before Mrs Simpson came onto the scene.

**I am the Love that dare not speak its name.**

LORD ALFRED DOUGLAS, 'Two Loves'

My Own Boy,
   Your sonnet is quite lovely, and it is a marvel that those red rose-petal lips of yours should have been made no less for music of song than for madness of kisses...

So commenced a letter from Oscar Wilde to his lover Lord Alfred Douglas. When a blackmailer named Allen got hold of the original, he offered it to Wilde in return for £10. Wilde replied: 'You have no appreciation of literature. If you had asked me for £50, I might have given it to you . . . I look upon it as a work of art.'

A few days later Allen called at Wilde's home to say that he had just been offered £60 for the letter. Wilde told him he should accept it. 'I myself have never received so large a sum for any work of that length, but I am glad to find there is someone in England who considers a letter of mine worth £60.' When the despairing Allen pleaded he was penniless, Wilde generously gave him ten shillings.

Shortly afterwards, the letter was returned to him by a colleague of Allen's, who complained it was no use trying to extort money out of Wilde because he only laughed at them. Wilde gave the man ten shillings, with the words, 'I'm afraid you are leading a wonderfully wicked life.'

'There's good and bad in all of us,' mumbled Allen's friend as he pocketed the money.

'You are a born philosopher,' said Wilde.

When Noël Coward was a teenager, he was encouraged by a mischievous pair of cousins to come to a party dressed as a girl. He looked so elegant in his long dress and craftily applied make-up that one young man at the party actually fell for him and invited 'her' out for a walk in the garden. When asked for a kiss, Noël gave him a playful look but pointed out that nice girls never went so far on a first meeting. Back indoors, Coward kept up the act so well that the eager admirer called round again the next morning. Somehow keeping their faces straight, the cousins informed him that the light of his life had already left; all they could do for him was pass on the letter which he gave them:

My Dear Little Flapper,

You can imagine my feelings when I arrived at the Bulteels' this morning, to find you had flown. I was fearfully sick as I was looking forward to spending an exceedingly pleasant morning with you on the lake and was beastly disappointed. I do call it real hard lines and I am still feeling beastly depressed. I have got a little remembrance of you which I am loath to part with – your cigarette holder. Am I to send it on to you? If so ... I will grudgingly do so. Will you let me write to you occasionally, and if so, will you answer my letters? Should I be presuming too much if I asked for your photo? I hope that you are not going to ignore me and forget me altogether.

With best love,
yours ever,
A. S.

'Miss' Coward enjoyed reading the letter, but could not bring himself to write back.

A handy excuse for not writing to a loved one was dreamed up by the poet John Betjeman, when his first fiancée Camilla Russell asked why he had not written to her for a month. 'It is the result of neither overwork nor annoyance but mere *episto-phobia*,' he told her. 'I love you, duckie, just the same.'

> **'Let us not speak, for the love we bear**
>    **one another —**
> **Let us hold hands and look.'**
> **She, such a very ordinary little woman;**
>    **He such a thumping crook;**
> **But both, for a moment, little lower than**
>    **the angels**
> **In the teashop's ingle-nook.**
>
> JOHN BETJEMAN 'In a Bath Teashop'

When naval service kept Vice-Admiral Nelson apart from his beloved Lady Hamilton, he could only convey his feelings for her by letter. However, the letters of every English serviceman were checked by the censors and the last thing Nelson wanted to do was make public his passion for the wife of the widely respected Sir William Hamilton. To fool the censors, Nelson pretended to be writing on behalf of an illiterate sailor named Thompson, whose wife was supposedly in Lady Hamilton's care. Through 'Thompson', all Nelson's feelings were revealed. Just as Lady Hamilton was expecting a child by her maritime lover, so was 'Mrs Thompson'. After the baby girl was born, Nelson (as Nelson) informed Mrs T., 'I cannot write, I am so agitated by this young man at my elbow. I believe he is foolish; he does nothing but rave about you and her.' But in the months that followed, Nelson dropped his guard. He could not hide his jealousy at the thought of Lady Hamilton hosting a dinner which the Prince of Wales, later to be crowned George IV, was to attend. 'Do not sit long at table . . .' Nelson wrote feverishly, 'he will be next to you, and telling you soft things . . . Oh God, that I was dead . . . He will put his foot near you . . .' As things turned out, Nelson needn't have worried – the dinner never happened.

Anne Boleyn kept Henry VIII dancing on a string by encouraging his advances, but never going 'all the way' to becoming his mistress. Her letters to him were full of promise; his letters to her were ardent and imploring. In the end, Anne's teasing drove Henry into a wild attempt to break the record for the longest ever sentence in a love letter:

I beseech you now with all my heart definitely to let me know your whole mind as to the love between us; for necessity compels me to plague you for a reply, having been for more than a year now struck by the dart of love, and being uncertain either of failure or of finding a place in your heart and affection, which point has certainly kept me for some time from naming you my mistress, since if you only love me with an ordinary love the name is not appropriate to you, seeing that it stands for an uncommon position very remote from the ordinary; but if it pleases you to do the duty of a true, loyal mistress and friend, and to give yourself body and heart to me, who have been and will be your very loyal servant (if your vigour does not forbid me) I promise you that not only the name will be due to you, but also to take you as my sole mistress, casting off all others than yourself out of mind and affection, and to serve you only . . .

Written by the hand of him who would willingly remain your
H. R.

Their eventual marriage lasted just three years. When Anne was accused of committing adultery with various members of the court, the King, in far fewer words, sentenced her to death.

Henry's father, Henry VII, enjoyed a far happier marriage. In 1492, he and his army were laying siege to the port of Boulogne, when he received a love letter from his wife, Elizabeth, which was so warm and affectionate that he promptly ended the siege and set sail for home.

The closest that the puritan Oliver Cromwell ever came to writing a love letter was after his victory at the Battle of Dunbar. 'Thou art dearer to me than any creature,' he informed his wife, Elizabeth, tempering this uncharacteristic rush of emotion with the words, 'let that suffice.'

What on earth could an attractive thirty-year-old female see in a wrinkled tap dancer well over twice her age? Ms Robyn Smith, scribbling this hasty note to Fred Astaire, wasn't sure either.

**Dear Fred, Thank you for dinner last week. I had a good time, and I miss seeing you, although I don't know why.**

Hopefully she found out before their wedding in 1980.

During the four years of his engagement to Martha Bernays, Sigmund Freud sent her almost a thousand letters. 'I know you are not beautiful in a painter's or sculptor's sense,' he wrote in one letter. 'If you insist on strict correctness in the use of words then I must confess you are not beautiful . . . What I meant to convey was how much the magic of your being expresses itself in your countenance and your body, how much there is visible in your appearance that reveals how sweet, generous and reasonable you are.'

Even in love, the analytical side of Freud's character shines through. Humphrey Bogart, writing to Lauren Bacall whilst he was still married to his hard-boozing wife Mayo, was more effusive. Beneath the tough exterior beat the heart of a true romantic.

I wish with all my heart that things were different – someday soon they will be. And now I know what was meant by 'To say goodbye is to die a little' – because when I walked away from you that last time and saw you standing there so darling I did die a little in my heart.

 **No one has ever written a romance better than we lived it.**

LAUREN BACALL

## YOURS FAITHFULLY . . .

Queen Mary, wife of William of Orange, addressed one letter, 'Dear, dear husband . . .' and signed it 'your dog on a string, your fish in a net, your bird in a cage, your humble trout, Mary.' Lovers call each other so many strange names that this letter would not appear especially remarkable, if it weren't for the fact that the queen was not writing to King William but to her female companion, Frances Apsley.

# WORDS OF LOVE

James Joyce, renowned for his often baffling literary works, made his feelings uncommonly clear in this letter to the light of his life, Nora Barnacle:

My dear Nora,

It has just struck me. I came in at half past eleven. Since then I have been sitting in an easy chair like a fool. I could do nothing. I hear nothing but your voice. I am like a fool hearing you call me 'Dear'. I offended two men today by leaving them coolly. I wanted to hear your voice, not theirs.

When I am with you I leave aside my contemptuous, suspicious nature. I wish I felt your head on my shoulder. I think I will go to bed.

I have been a half-hour writing this thing. Will you write something to me? I hope you will. How am I to sign myself? I won't sign anything at all, because I don't know what to sign myself.

Well, what did you expect – 'Love Jim, XXX'?

# CHAPTER FOUR

# THE THOUGHT THAT COUNTS

*Gifts from admirers —
and the odd wedding present*

Fidel Castro, Cuba's socialist leader for the past thirty years, is the last person one would expect to pay much regard for material possessions, but a year or two before his overthrow of the Batista regime he splashed out with uncommon extravagance on an eighteen-year-old girl named Isabelle Custodio. Already divorced from his first wife, Castro proposed marriage to her, with promises of a more exciting life than the one she was currently leading behind the counter of a record shop. The couple drifted apart before the wedding could take place, but of the gifts he showered on her beforehand, the most unwanted was a single-piece swimming costume. Isabelle already owned a most becoming bikini, thank you very much. This, of course, was the problem. The sight of Isabelle's lovely brown stomach was one thing Fidel did not want to share with the Cuban people.

Bikinis came too late for Queen Victoria to try one on, but she may not have been so prudish about the idea as most people would expect. Amongst the presents she gave to her beloved Albert on their wedding day was a nude painting of the goddess Artemis. Whatever happened to Victorian values?

Before coming to the throne, and a couple of years before her marriage, our own monarch showed more discretion than her great-great-grandmother by enclosing a photograph of herself fully clothed in a Christmas card to Lieutenant Philip Mountbatten. In return, the young, dashing sailor sent her one of himself, which still stands framed on the Queen's writing desk at Buckingham Palace.

When Princess Elizabeth and Prince Philip married in 1947, wedding presents arrived at the Palace from all corners of the world. Probably the most curious gift was a cloth which Mahatma Gandhi had woven for the royal couple with his own bare hands. There is some dispute as to whether it was designed to go under a tray or was in fact a loincloth. Mary, the Queen Mother, clearly thought the latter. 'How indelicate!' she exclaimed. 'What a horrible thing!' Prince Philip, showing the kind of tact for which he is not especially renowned, tried to drown her cries with a short but loud declaration of the Mahatma's undoubted greatness.

> 66
>
> **I think everybody will concede that on this, of all days, I should begin my speech with the words 'My husband and I'.**
>
> QUEEN ELIZABETH II
> 26 November 1972 (her twenty-fifth wedding anniversary)

Franz Liszt showed no tact, but a decidedly scheming side to his nature, when he gave a copy of the George Sand novel *Lélia* to Countess Marie d'Agoult. The book was famous in its time for questioning the institution of marriage and for its plucky heroine, who demands her freedom if her husband cannot fulfil her physical needs.

Uncoincidentally, Countess Marie d'Agoult had just left her rather unexciting husband to set up home with Liszt.

If it *is* the thought that counts, actress Tippi Hedren would rather not have known what was going through Alfred Hitchcock's mind when he gave her five-year-old daughter a doll to play with. The doll was dressed exactly as Tippi had been when starring in Hitchcock's film *The Birds*. It was bad enough to be reminded of that experience, when the actress had had live birds tied to her, pecking at her body to give the film its frightening realism, but where Hitchcock really blew any lingering hopes of winning Tippi's heart was in the packaging of the doll: little Miss Hedren's 'mummy' was presented to her lying in its own little coffin.

Speakin' of coughin' . . . If smoking seriously damages your health, a cigarette case would seem to be an odd sort of present to give to someone you loved. The romance, though, lies in the inscription. In the first film they made together, *To Have and Have Not*, Lauren Bacall gave Humphrey Bogart a famous lesson in the art of whistling. Soon after their wedding, Bogart presented his young wife with a cigarette case inscribed with the words: 'For Mrs Me, who need never whistle for Bogie.'

Another lady with whom Sinatra stepped out for a while was Marilyn Monroe. When she separated from playwright Arthur Miller, it was Miller who retained custody of Hugo, a basset hound that Marilyn also loved. To ease the pain of this separation, Frank thoughtfully gave her a white poodle. A grateful Marilyn called her new pet 'Maf'.

If it weren't for a lover's thoughtfulness, there would only have been Six Wonders of the World. After leaving her family and friends in the mountains of north-west Iran, King Nebuchadnezzar's wife Amuhea felt so homesick that the King knocked up a little something to cheer her up – the Hanging Gardens of Babylon.

Catherine the Great of Russia came to power by conspiring with her lover Grigori Orlov to depose her husband Tsar Peter III. Peter was imprisoned and, soon after, assassinated. If no one dared point the finger at Catherine, she certainly did well out of his demise, ruling Russia for the next thirty-four years and sleeping with the pick of Russia's thrusting young men (after they had been tested for VD and tried out in bed by a hardworking noblewoman in Catherine's court). Besides the threat of instant castration or death or both if they refused, her lovers always found it worth their while, as Catherine showed her appreciation in thousands of roubles and mountains of diamonds. When she eventually dropped her old conniver Orlov, his golden handshake included a silver dinner service and seven thousand serfs! Orlov's successor, a young officer named Potemkin also did quite well, picking up the titles of Prince, Field Marshal and Grand Admiral of the Black Sea, not to mention Battleship. On one occasion Catherine presented Potemkin with four magnificent watches, for which he was so grateful that he wore them all at the same time.

> **This diamond has so many carats, it's almost a turnip.**
>
> RICHARD BURTON

## THE THOUGHT THAT COUNTS

During his affairs with Elizabeth Taylor, Richard Burton enjoyed dishing out diamonds almost as plentifully as Catherine the Great. One of the cheaper ones he got her was for her fortieth birthday, costing a mere fifty thousand dollars (at 1972 prices!). Heart-shaped, it had been designed by the same man who had built the Taj Mahal. 'I would have liked to have bought the Taj Mahal for Elizabeth,' said the tightfisted Burton, 'but it would have cost too much to transport it.'

The most important thing to remember when buying jewellery for your loved one is to make sure it goes to the right person. Charles Dickens' marriage was already on the rocks – he and his wife, Catherine, were sleeping in separate bedrooms – when Dickens started his liaison with an actress named Ellen Ternan. Nevertheless, it was a spectacular blunder on the part of the jewellers when a bracelet which Dickens had ordered for Ellen was instead delivered to his wife. The marriage was far too far beyond repair for Dickens to pretend he'd bought it for Catherine.

Composer Richard Wagner celebrated the birth of his son by dedicating the 'Siegfried Idyll' to his wife Cosima. When a friend mentioned this fact to Walt Disney, Walt thought it was such a great idea that he would dedicate his next film to *his* wife. The gift was not exactly Wagnerian in scale, but presumably his wife managed to come up with a smile on being presented with *The Three Little Pigs*.

## IF YOU CAN'T MAKE A PRESENT GOOD, AT LEAST MAKE IT PRACTICAL...

Johnny Weissmuller's wife Lupe Velez, a keen boxing fan, was known for her flying fists whenever conversation took an unfriendly turn. On marrying Hollywood's 'Tarzan' she gave him a pair of boxing gloves, with instructions to punch some sense into her if she ever tried to leave him.

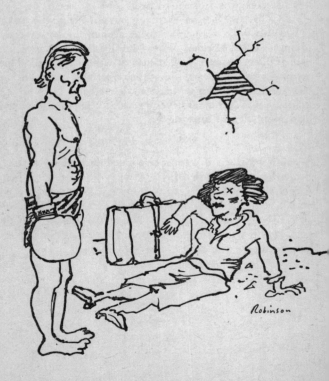

Why did Elvis Presley give Jayne Mansfield a pink motorbike? There's nothing mysterious about the choice of colour, as everything in the Hollywood bombshell's home was pink, from her kettle to her Cadillac. Jayne, the proud owner of a heart-shaped bed and heart-shaped swimming pool, was making a film called *The Girl Can't Help It* when Mr Presley came to stay. The story goes that she slept with Elvis hoping that he would then agree to sing in the film free of charge. But Elvis didn't surrender a fee that easily and the next morning they tossed a coin for it. Jayne lost the toss and Elvis took his fee, but sportingly spent part of it on the bike.

Another couple in the transports of passion were Jane Fonda and French film director Roger Vadim. During their marriage, Jane was far keener than Roger on the idea of children, so in the end they struck a deal. 'I'll give you a baby,' said Vadim, 'if you give me a red Ferrari.' 'OK,' said Jane. In fact she gave him a blue one, but Vadim generously overlooked this detail and donated the necessary seed.

## SAY IT WITH FLOWERS . . .

**" I still bring my wife flowers; you have to do that. What the blazes did you get married for if you're prepared to let the romance in your life disappear?**

TERRY WOGAN

Having decided that she wanted to spend a weekend on her own, opera star Kiri Te Kanawa resorted to a popular trick to keep her boyfriend Desmond at bay. When Des rang her flat, Kiri got a friend to answer it and say she was out. Desmond responded by sending her a huge bouquet of flowers. From then on, their love blossomed and they married in August of the same year, 1967. Only later did Desmond tell her how close he had come to sending a farewell letter with the flowers.

Proving that he could romance right up there with the best of them, Sigmund Freud sent a single red rose every day to his wife-to-be, Martha. Along with each rose was a card, written – according to Freud's mood – in German, English, Spanish or Latin.

What could be more romantic than to keep a lock of your lover's hair close to your heart? In answering that question, Lady Caroline Lamb came up with a more Freudian gift than Freud ever gave. Aware that the poet Byron's passion for her was cooling, she tried to rekindle the flame by snipping off a locket's worth of her hair and sending it for him to treasure. However, the hairs were not from her *head*! Lord Byron, clearly unimpressed by the short and curly specimens, declined her request for a clump from his own groin and took another lover.

Fidel Castro's relationship with young Isabelle may have petered out to nothing, but he gained another admirer in Isabelle's guardian, Teresa. Teresa was particularly impressed with his calm, noble manner, likening him to 'a big New-foundland dog'. On his twenty-ninth birthday she presented him with a German razor which she knew he was taken with. He thanked her profusely; it was, he told her, the only present he had been given and he swore he would keep it for ever. However, it was at about this time that he started to grow his famous beard. The precious razor has remained almost totally unused.

# CHAPTER FIVE

# THE THINGS WE DO FOR LOVE

## Tales of scheming, sacrifice and something else beginning with 's'

*T*erry *Wogan told a little lie to win his lady, King David resorted to more fatal methods to win his – the history of underhand games in the name of love spans the history of mankind, from Biblical Times to Radio Times.*

**K**ing David's main claim to fame is the slingshot that slew Goliath, but he was also something of a ladykiller. One day, from the roof of his palace, he spotted the beautiful Bathsheba bathing and – in the way kings do – instantly summoned her. With her husband Uriah away at war, their affair was going very smoothly until she broke the news to David that she was pregnant. In a vain attempt to keep a lid on things, David called Uriah back from the front for a full report on how the war was going. The real reason, of course, was to give Uriah the chance to sleep with Bathsheba and thus account for her pregnancy. However, during wartime, it was the custom for soldiers to abstain from sex so as not to sap their strength. Uriah, a fine military man, observed the custom, even after an increasingly desperate David had got him drunk. In the end, David packed him back off to war. His farewell present to Uriah was a sealed message to his commander, instructing him to send Uriah into the very thick of the battle. News soon came of Uriah's death and David married Bathsheba.

Happily, the deception was on a smaller scale (and free of bloodshed) when Terry Wogan engineered a date with a pretty model called Helen Joyce. A few days after meeting her at a party, young Tel phoned her to say that his parents had bought some tickets for a musical but now couldn't make it; would she like to come? Helen said she would. On the night, they found their view severely restricted by a pillar in front of them. Still, there was no point in Terry or his future wife complaining to his parents about their seats — Terry had bought the tickets himself.

> **When my love swears she is made of truth,**
> **I do believe her, though I know she lies.**
> WILLIAM SHAKESPEARE

Of course, anyone who chooses to be economical with the truth cannot afford to be too disgusted when the tables are turned. 'Bad' King John, like many a monarch before and since, had an eye for the ladies and went to extraordinary lengths to ensnare them. When he decided he wanted to seduce the wife of a nobleman named de Vesci, he borrowed the man's ring and sent it to her home with the message that de Vesci was dying and she was to come to see the king immediately. However, on her way to London, she met her husband coming the other way. When they realized what John was up to, they sent a prostitute along in her place. The next day, John smiled smugly at de Vesci and said, 'Your wife is very pleasant in the silence of the night.' De Vesci, returning the King's smile, nodded in agreement and then informed him of the swap. Remarkably, he lived to tell the tale.

When it comes to the crunch, few people find love is worth dying for. For carrying on a secret affair with a Roman Emperor's wife, the best one could hope for was that the execution would be quick and not involve too many wild

Robinson

animals. Mnester, a dancer during the rule of Claudius, certainly didn't fancy that fate half as much as the emperor's wife fancied *him*. The Emperess Messalina even had statues of Mnester put up all over Rome in her efforts to win his heart. When this didn't work, she went to Claudius and complained that Mnester was being unco-operative over quite a different matter. Claudius summoned Mnester and told him that he should show more respect to Rome's first lady and obey her every command. So, the next time Messalina propositioned him, the loyal Mnester did his duty.

> **In love, men are amateurs, women the professionals.**
>
> FRANÇOIS TRUFFAUT

T. S. Eliot's second wife, Valerie, was just fourteen when her heart was moved by a recording of one of Eliot's poems, 'The Journey of the Magi'. From that moment, she knew she simply had to meet the man behind the work. Her first job after leaving school was as secretary to a writer, but she had been working for him for only a year when she heard through a friend that Eliot himself was looking for a secretary. According to Valerie, Eliot was as nervous in the interview as she was, but she got the job and – in the end – her man. Eight years after the interview, in the romantic setting of Faber & Faber's offices, he proposed to her.

Singer-songwriter Carole King was living next door to Ryan O'Neal when she hit upon a subtle way of getting him over to her place. She wrote a song about a hunk of a neighbour and how much she'd love to get to know him. As soon as he heard the record, Ryan was ringing her bell to borrow some sugar.

What these 'just good neighbours' really needed was a contraption along the lines of King Louis XV's 'Flying Chair'. When it came to finding ways of filling the royal time, Louis had difficulty thinking up any alternatives to making love. His wife Maria had ten children and complained she was either 'in bed, pregnant or brought to bed!' Another favourite, Madame de Pompadour, tried all kinds of alleged aphrodisiacs, such as truffles, celery and vanilla, but she couldn't keep up either. The 'Flying Chair' was an invention of Louis' which involved a pulley system by which he could be hoisted in a chair up to his mistress's rooms on the floor above. By avoiding all the bother of walking up the stairs himself, Louis was able to conserve his energy for the bed. Besides the invention of the 'Flying Chair', probably his wisest act was to die in 1774, before the French Revolution could come and spoil his fun.

> 66 **Love is like the measles; we all have to go through it.**
>
> JEROME K. JEROME

Walt Disney had never been all that keen on tennis until he learned that his attractive classmate Su Pitowski was a regular player. As it was his only motivation for taking up the game, it came as a severe blow to find that girls and boys had to play on separate courts. They never did play together, although the thought that she may be watching inspired a steady improvement in the Disney backhand. Whatever Su thought of his tennis, she accepted when Disney asked her out. The relationship only cooled when Walt went off to France to serve in the Red Cross at the end of the First World War. They exchanged letters while he was away, but one fact that she failed to mention before he came back was that she had married someone else.

French composer Hector Berlioz's most famous work, the *Symphonie Fantastique*, is a love story set to music, inspired by his infatuation with the actress Harriet Smithson, to whom he sent ardent letters of unbridled passion before they'd even met! The symphony starts in a romantic vein but then, since Ms Smithson was understandably hesitant in returning his affections, Berlioz expressed his anguish by depicting his own execution in the fourth movement, and, in the finale, portraying his once beloved Harriet as a whore attending a witches' Sabbath. After six years of intensive wooing, Harriet finally gave in and they embarked on a rather unhappy marriage.

> ❝ **One is very crazy when one is in love.**
> SIGMUND FREUD

Berlioz may not have believed it, but usually there does come a point when a sane person has to take no for an answer. One woman was so determined to get her hands on film idol Omar Sharif that she burst into his hotel room with a gun and insisted he took his clothes off. While Omar reluctantly obliged, she did the same and then lay on the bed. But her daring plan came to nothing. One-night stands had never been Sharif's scene and, even if they had been, waving a gun at a man's private parts is a sure-fire way to cool the mightiest ardour. As the naked Omar politely pointed out, he was simply not up to the task.

Alma, the wife of Gustav Mahler, was herself a promising composer until her career was cut short by her egocentric husband. Before their marriage, Alma sent him a letter saying she wouldn't be able to write to him for a while as she had to concentrate on her composition. Gustav flew into a rage and wrote straight back, demanding she give up composing and devote herself to supporting him. Remarkably, Alma consented, though not without tears. The sacrifice of her own creative fulfilment was to be a constant cause of tension between them. But Mahler was so wrapped up in being a genius that several years passed before he realized just how great a sacrifice it had been. When the penny dropped, he was so stricken with guilt that he became, for a while, impotent. He was only cured after a session on the psychiatrist's couch with Sigmund Freud. The next Alma knew, her husband was playing her songs (unheard for ten years) in their house, and their relationship – and love life – hit new heights.

> ❝ **There is no such thing as love. There are only proofs of love.**
>
> PABLO PICASSO

Anne of Denmark tried to make a success of her marriage to James I by joining him in his favourite pursuits, one of which was hunting. But the plan tragically backfired when, out on a hunt, she accidentally shot the King's favourite hound, Jewel.

'Don't go changing to try to please me . . .' Not every romance is as perfect as the one conjured up by Billy Joel's song 'Just the Way You Are'. Sometimes there are just one or two changes which you wouldn't mind your partner making. The mildly dotty Lady Caroline Lamb was no one's idea of the perfect wife, but she was at least aware that her behaviour left room for improvement. Occasionally she would resolve to change. 'I will be silent of a morning,' she promised her long-suffering husband William Lamb, 'entertaining after dinner, docile, fearless as a heroine in the last volume of her troubles, and strong as a mountain tiger.' It is not known whether this plan lasted twenty-four hours or less. The marriage lasted twenty years, until relatives thoughtfully organized a formal separation.

Prime Minister Benjamin Disraeli's wife Mary showed selflessness way beyond the call of duty on the day he was due to deliver a very important speech. They were getting into the carriage to travel to the venue together when Mary caught her hand in the closing door. Rather than let out a cry of pain, she bit her lip and remained silent for the whole of the ride, leaving her husband free to concentrate, undisturbed, on the speech ahead.

> **Love is blind, and lovers cannot see The pretty follies that themselves commit.**
>
> WILLIAM SHAKESPEARE *The Merchant of Venice*

An ex-porn-movie star named Joyce McKinney enjoyed her fifteen minutes of fame in 1977 when she kidnapped a Mormon missionary called Kirk Anderson. The reason why this mild-mannered Mormon became the object of her obsession was, according to Joyce, that he was the only man she had ever met who didn't want to sleep with her. She had even the most quote-hungry of reporters choking, when she announced that 'for the love of Kirk I'd have skied down Everest in the nude with a carnation up my nose'. Abducting him from church and keeping him chained to a bed for three days was, presumably, less strenuous and not so cold.

> **I swear I will be faithful; I could be trusted with fifty virgins naked in a dark room.**
>
> HORATIO NELSON (to Lady Hamilton)

There *are* easier ways to impress a lover. Nevertheless, physical feats should be attempted with caution, even when fully clothed. When Nigel Mansell and wife Roseanne were courting, Nigel kept his eyes open for opportunities to show her what a wonderful guy he was. Once when they were out walking in Wales, they came to a point where a few feet of seawater separated them from the next piece of land. Eager to impress, Mansell offered to leap across it and then catch Roseanne when *she* jumped. Our hero paced out his run-up, then charged. The full meaning of the proverb 'Look Before You Leap' must have hit him somewhere between take-off and the cold, choppy water. 'A few feet' turned out to be more like twenty. The resultant splash was greatly appreciated by Roseanne and a small crowd of onlookers.

# CHAPTER SIX

# WIN SOME, LOSE SOME

## Proposals, proper and improper, accepted and rejected

*That moment when you propose or are proposed to is one you never forget – a once, twice or (as the divorce rate rises) thrice in a lifetime experience. Not many people would expect to match the fifty proposals that Barbara Cartland received before finally saying yes, let alone the* twelve a day *that Liberace received at the height of his popularity. It is also to be hoped that few will have to suffer twelve rejections, as William IV did before striking it thirteenth time lucky.*

Traditionally, proposing is seen as the man's job, with women only taking the initiative once every four years, on 29 February. But there have always been exceptions to this sexist (and slowly changing?) state of affairs. A hundred and fifty years ago, it was Queen Victoria who popped the question to Albert. Her diary entry for the big day reflects her joy and relief at his acceptance: 'I said to him that I thought he must be aware *why* I wished him to come here, and that it would make me *too happy* if he would consent to what I wished (to marry me); we embraced each other over and over again, and he was *so* kind, *so* affectionate; Oh! to *feel* I was, and am, loved by *such* an Angel as Albert was *too great delight to describe*! he is *perfection*; perfection in every way – in beauty – in everything! I told him I was quite unworthy of him and kissed his hand . . . no two Lovers could ever be happier than we are!'

'Mrs Livingstone, I presume?' Brought up in the African jungle by missionary parents, Mary Moffat had seen her share of wild beasts, but none at the close quarters experienced by her friend Dr David Livingstone when he went on a lion hunt with African natives and ended up being mauled by the lion. His arm was still in a sling when he paid her a visit in the Kuruman Valley and proposed to her. In such a romantic setting, a sultry African orchard by a stream, how could she turn down this rugged doctor who had wrestled with a lion and then, braving the pain, set his broken arm himself? They were married for seventeen years, till Mary died of jungle fever.

## MAJOR MARRIAGE PROBLEM FOR J. R.

Larry Hagman – J. R. from Dallas – has been happily married for nearly forty years to a Swedish lady named Maj (pronounced 'my'). The down-to-earth setting for his proposal was the middle of a muddy field. Larry was doing his stint in the US Air Force, organizing shows for the troops throughout Europe, when he took young Maj out for a drive. When they strayed off the main road, the car got unexpectedly bogged down. They were sitting waiting for a tractor to come and pull them out, when J. R. broke the silence. 'I hadn't planned to do it this way, Maj, but will you marry me?' 'Sure,' she replied. But Larry's commanding officer was not so sure. In fact, he refused to give his permission. When Larry asked why, he was informed that it was against regulations for him to marry a major. Once that little misunderstanding had been tidied up, they married, on Larry's twenty-third birthday.

> **For a long time I thought *coq au vin* meant love in a lorry.**
>
> VICTORIA WOOD

Young American couples get up to so much in their automobiles that it must seem a natural place to propose marriage. When Walt Disney took his girlfriend Lillian out in his battered old Ford, he was wearing a brand new suit and proudly asked her what she thought of it. Well, Lillian replied, much as she liked the suit, she couldn't help feeling that its main effect was to emphasize the shabbiness of the car. The next evening, Walt took her out again and told her she was right, the car was a wreck. But times were hard; he needed Lillian's advice. Which would she prefer him to buy, a new car for both of them or an engagement ring for her? Lillian opted for the ring. Years later, she remarked to her daughter, 'He seemed quite disappointed I didn't let him buy the car.'

It was wise of Disney to offer a choice; had Lillian turned him down, a new car would have provided some consolation. The choice put to Sarah Bernhardt by her lover, Henri, Prince de Ligne, was not so sensible. Sarah had yet to become one of the stage's most famous actresses when Henri proposed marriage in the form of an ultimatum: 'Love me and leave the stage, or leave me.' Henri had clearly not bargained for Sarah's overpowering love of the theatre, as he soon found himself without a mistress.

Of all forms of proposal, the brusque ultimatum must be the most likely to fail. The first man to propose marriage to

Agatha Christie was a no-nonsense colonel in the 17th Lancers, some fifteen years older than young Agatha. Though she was flattered by the proposal, she also sensed that something was missing. Sharing her daughter's doubts, Agatha's mum informed the suitor that he should not write or call on her for six months, after which they could reassess the situation. As soon as the six months were up, the colonel sent Agatha a telegram: 'Cannot stand this indecision any longer. Will you marry me, yes or no?' This, one of the most unromantic proposals ever dispatched, got the answer it deserved: 'No.'

Many of the girls who shared Errol Flynn's bed must have dreamed that the liaison would lead to marriage, but none of them had the flamboyant style of Lili Damita, a young French actress, who climbed out of the bedroom window, several floors up and told Flynn that she would jump unless he agreed to marry her. Flynn enjoyed a joke, and cheerfully embarked on the first of his three marriages.

**66 In each year with him I packed in more fun, more real living than some wives get in forty years.**
PATRICIA WYMORE (third wife of Errol Flynn)

The impulsive proposal is not recommended, but it can just occasionally work wonders. Prince Charles's favourite all-girl group, the Three Degrees, were on tour and bemoaning the way their work prevented them from getting to know any men, when one Degree, Sheila, made a decision. She was going to pick up the next man she saw. At that moment a cool hunk in a tuxedo popped his head round their dressing-room door. Sheila smiled approvingly and asked him, bluntly, if he played around. He replied by asking for a kiss. 'Only when we're engaged!' Sheila laughed, at which the man pulled the

ring off a can of Coke and put it on her finger. They kissed and, believe it or not, later married.

Almost as quick off the mark was Clive Dunn, Corporal Jones of 'Dad's Army' fame, who proposed to his second wife, an actress named Cilla, within twenty-four hours of meeting her. She accepted and was soon on the phone to her mother. On hearing that Mr Right was a comedian almost fifteen years Cilla's senior, her mum got straight to the heart of the matter. 'Is he funny?' she asked.

Love at first sight is not an unknown phenomenon. Engagement at first sight is rather rarer. Harry Cohn, the Hollywood studio chief who had built Kim Novak up into a star, was far from pleased to see her name regularly linked with that of Sammy Davis Jr. In those days, being attached to a black man was still regarded as a risk to a white actress's popularity. The story goes that Sammy Davis was driven into the desert by a couple of heavies who, alluding to his glass eye, made him an offer he couldn't refuse: 'Sammy, you got one eye left. Wanna keep it?' In return for his sight, all Sammy had to do was marry a black girl within twenty-four hours. That night, at a club called the Silver Slipper, a gorgeous black dancer named Loray White was knocked out of her stride by the legendary Mr Davis leaping up on to the stage and proposing to her. They had never met before. After six months of unconsummated 'marriage', they separated, with Loray $25,000 richer for her trouble.

In sixteenth-century Russia, a marriage proposal from Ivan the Terrible would have been enough to set any girl's heart a-pounding, but not with the happy anticipation that precedes today's royal weddings. The massacre of men, women and children came easily to Ivan and if anyone was foolish enough to say something he didn't want to hear, they could count themselves lucky if they just had their tongues cut out. To turn down an offer of marriage to this madman might therefore have been a touch risky. The first woman to say yes is acknowledged to have calmed the more bloodthirsty side of his nature, but when, after thirteen years, she died on him, he quickly reverted to his old ways, throwing people into the bear-pit just for laughs and stabbing the occasional jester. A second wife and several debauched virgins later, he selected the lucky girl who was to be Wife Number Three. Understandably, she swooned at the news and, perhaps equally understandably, never got up, having died of shock.

George Bernard Shaw suffered marginally less discomfort when Charlotte Payne-Townsend, who considered him the most self-centred man she had ever met, proposed to him in July 1897. If Shaw's letter to Ellen Terry is to be believed, her proposal filled him with a 'shuddering horror' and he 'wildly asked the fare to Australia'. But there was no escape. Within a year they had embarked on 'the terrible adventure' of marriage.

Marriage would probably have been a 'terrible adventure' for Felice Bauer if she had ever got hitched with Franz Kafka. One Christmas, when she suggested they meet up, Kafka insisted that he use his spare days away from the office to do some writing. Felice reluctantly made other plans, leaving Franz free to spend the holiday putting pen to paper ... writing letters to Felice! Unsurprisingly, a proposal of marriage from such an angst-ridden writer could never be interpreted as an offer of eternally shared bliss. As he wrote to Felice: 'Marry me, and you will regret it; marry me not, and you will regret it; marry me or marry me not, and you will regret either.' He died a bachelor.

> **Should I marry W.? Not if she won't tell me the other letters in her name . . .**
>
> WOODY ALLEN

George Orwell, aged forty-three and suffering from tuberculosis and bronchiectasis, knew that he was no girl's idea of a good catch. When he proposed to three women in fairly swift succession, he went to great pains to set out the disadvantages of marrying him. Besides his illness and the fact that he was several years older than each candidate, he was also convinced that he was sterile, although this had never been proven as he was unwilling to subject himself to such a 'disgusting' examination. Still, on the plus side, 'if you think of yourself as essentially a widow, then you might do worse'. The first of these three girls was Sonia Brownwell; a couple of years later, at the second time of asking, she accepted. He married her from his hospital bed in University College Hospital, London. Within four months, as predicted, Sonia was a widow.

Persistence sometimes pays. Matilda of Flanders turned down William the Conqueror's first proposal of marriage because he was a bastard. If she originally meant this in its literal sense, William's parents being unmarried, she soon found other reasons for calling him one – he was so angry at her refusal that he pestered her for the next seven years, dragging her around by the hair, beating her up and, on one occasion, knocking her off her horse into a pool of mud. At last she relented and, when asked how she could marry such a \*\*\*\*\*\*\*, she replied that only a man of great courage would dare to beat her up in her father's own palace.

Though not on the epic scale of William and Matilda's, the engagement between David Lloyd George and Margaret

Owen was more than a simple matter of proposal and acceptance. When Lloyd George proposed to her, it was his dashing good looks and charm that made Margaret hesitate; he had to be the unfaithful type, didn't he? When she revealed the reason for her doubts, he wrote to her, 'which would you prefer, a namby pamby who would always be hanging at the hem of your petticoat, or a real demon, though he would sometimes lose his temper with you? Tell me the truth, Maggie.'

Maggie's reply was written in the light of a fresh rumour, that Lloyd George was having an affair with another local girl. Perhaps, she suggested, he had accidentally proposed to the wrong woman.

Lloyd George shot a letter back. 'I have made my choice, I must ask you to make yours. We must settle this miserable squabble once and for all.'

The 'miserable squabble' ended in marriage. A few years later, whilst bringing up their family in Wales, Maggie can't have been too surprised when she learned that her husband was carrying on with his secretary in London.

Some thirty years before becoming one of Britain's great Prime Ministers, William Gladstone fell head over heels in love with the sister of an old Eton schoolfriend. Her name was Caroline Farquhar. Desperate to marry her, Gladstone wrote a long letter to Caroline's father, ruminating on his own destiny and the sort of future he could offer Caroline, if only Mr Farquhar would grant them permission to wed. Mr Farquhar stalled him for a while, but in the end it was left to Caroline's brother to break the news to his old schoolchum – Gladstone had been somewhat hasty. Before telling Caroline's father of his love and his plans, he should have had a word with Caroline herself; the fact was she didn't love him.

Many famous men have had to taste the bitter pill of rejection. William IV was turned down twelve times before he found a wife. Having served in the Navy from the age of thirteen until he was twenty-three, 'Sailor Billy' (or, sometimes, 'Silly Billy') was renowned for his coarse language and whoring habits, which diminished his appeal as a prospective husband. 'Oh for England,' he once wrote to his brother, 'and the pretty girls of Westminster, at least to such as would not clap or pox me every time we fucked.' In the end, the plain-featured and morbidly religious Princess Adelaide of Saxe-Coburg-Meiningen took her place in history by agreeing to marry the last King of England (on record!) to have suffered from VD.

At the other end of the proposals scale was twinkling pianist Liberace, whose average of twelve proposals a week included one from a hopeful lady offering $200,000 as part of her dowry. Unfortunately for her, this was little incentive to a star who was gaily earning over a million dollars a year in appearance money alone.

## WIN SOME, LOSE SOME

Beethoven often talked with his male friends about women and marriage, but sadly for him he died a bachelor. Each proposal of marriage he made was rejected; one wife-not-to-be was a well-known singer named Magdelena Willman, who confided to a friend that she had turned him down 'because he was so ugly – and half mad'.

> **Marriage has many pains, but celibacy has no pleasures.**
>
> DR JOHNSON

> **I don't miss having a sex life . . . I'd rather have a cup of tea and a good conversation.**
>
> BOY GEORGE

Robinson

Even though the proposer must steel him- or herself for rejection, it does help if the person doing the rejecting exercises a little sensitivity. One example not to follow is that of Lady Mary Wortley Montagu, who, when proposed to by the writer Alexander Pope, burst into uncontrollable laughter. From that moment, Pope was transformed from ardent admirer to sworn enemy.

Tippi Hedren, star of *The Birds* and *Marnie*, had already told director Alfred Hitchcock that she was going to marry her agent once the shooting of *Marnie* was over. Nevertheless, Hitchcock insisted on proposing to her in her trailer and, when she reminded him of her other plans, he threatened to end her movie career unless she changed her mind. Tippi, having been tied to the floor and been pecked by live seagulls in *The Birds*, must have reckoned that the end of her movie career might not be such a bad thing. She remained adamant: No, she would not marry him. Hitchcock (who, it so happened, was already married at the time) never spoke to her again. For the rest of the movie, any direction he wanted to give her was passed on via an assistant.

The Catherine Wheel firework takes its name from Saint Catherine of Alexandria, who rose to fame for protesting the public worship of idols and arguing her case successfully against fifty of the finest philosophers in the land. The Emperor Maxentius was impressed and proposed marriage, but she turned him down. Maxentius took it badly, having her imprisoned, beaten and then displayed in public, tied to a large wheel. When the wheel suddenly fell apart (probably due to shoddy workmanship), several spectators were injured but two hundred soldiers were instantly converted and – almost as instantly – beheaded, along with Catherine.

Even when a proposal *is* accepted, there is still a long way to go before the couple walk hand in hand out of the church or Register Office. A beautiful pianist named Maria Wodzinski was delighted to accept when Frédéric Chopin proposed to her in July 1836. However her parents could not share her joy, knowing Chopin's reputation for making the most of Parisian nightlife. The great composer was put on probation; if he managed to lead a quieter life for an agreed length of time, the marriage could go ahead. Chopin left Paris for a while, but on his return he either forgot about the curfew or found the social whirl irresistible. The Wodzinskis reached a verdict; he was not the man for Maria. In sudden desperation he flooded them with gifts and letters, but to no avail. He had blown it; all he could do now was tie his letters from Maria into a bundle marked 'My miseries', and try to forget her.

'I ought to tell you that I proposed to a jolly girl last week and got accepted. It has left me rather dippy . . .' So John Betjeman wrote to his friend Patrick Balfour after proposing to Camilla Russell, a girl whose father happened to be head of the Cairo police force. The engagement would never have lasted long, as both soon found themselves attracted to alternative partners, but it was in fact a gift from Betjeman to Camilla that sealed their fate. The novel *Boy* by James Hanley was, to some commentators, a rumbustious tale of life on the ocean waves but to the Cairo chief of police it was nothing other than 'pornographic'. As soon as he learned of the gift, he insisted on the immediate termination of their engagement.

Barbara Cartland, Queen of Romantic Bestsellers, has sold more books than any other writer – over 350 million in the world. Another record may be the number of proposals she received before finally marrying Alexander McCorquodale, a

Scottish printer. He was the fiftieth man to have gone down on one knee for her. However, it was not the first proposal she had ever *accepted*. For a while she was secretly engaged to a Life Guards officer named Dick Usher, but before the official announcement appeared in *The Times*, Barbara happened to ask her mother where babies came from; up till then all she knew was that a bit of kissing was involved. When her mum broke the news about sex, Barbara, disgusted, broke off the engagement.

# CHAPTER SEVEN

# BEYOND REACH

*Loves platonic, unrequited,
and impossible*

> **You can give me money, yes, but you
> cannot give me a wife and child!**
> VINCENT VAN GOGH (letter to brother Theo)

The love life of Vincent Van Gogh was as highly charged
and ill-fated as the rest of his existence. Both the great 'loves'
of his life were unable to return his passion. The first of these
was a girl called Ursula, the daughter of Van Gogh's landlady
in London. Since Ursula worked in a crèche, Vincent saw her
as 'the angel surrounded by babies'. Vincent couldn't believe
his luck that they both lived under the same roof; Ursula,
whilst enjoying the attention he lavished on her, didn't share
his sense of good fortune. When at last, in a romantic frenzy,
he declared his love for her, she burst out laughing and told
him she was already engaged. Several times he begged her to
break it off, but each time her response was laughter. He had
no more luck five years later, when he fell for a widowed
cousin named Kee. 'No, never, never!' was her reply when
Van Gogh proposed to her. But it always took more than one
rejection to see off Vincent. Kee escaped to her parents' home,
only for Vincent to turn up on their doorstep to propose
again. In the end, Kee's father told Vincent bluntly to forget

the whole affair. At which Vincent reached for a lamp and held his hand over the flame, declaring he would not pull it away until Kee came to see him. Kee's father promptly blew the flame out and sent Vincent packing. 'At that,' Vincent wrote to brother Theo, 'I felt my love die ... A void, an immense void, has opened up in my heart.'

The flame of passion was extinguished in more startling fashion by Anton Dolin, a young ballet dancer who had caught the eye of the writer Somerset Maugham. It was at one of Ivor Novello's parties in a suite at the Savoy that Maugham propositioned Dolin: 'L–let me t–take you home,' he stuttered. Anton politely declined, even after Novello had told him, only half in jest, that acceptance would probably get him a gold Cartier cigarette case the next morning. Later that night, Dolin was in bed, alone, when he was woken by a violent knocking. From his bedroom window he looked down into the street to see a drunken Maugham still hammering at his door. The hammering only stopped when Dolin cooled the author's ardour with the contents of his chamberpot, emptied out of the window and on to his head.

" **A man marries to have a home, but also because he doesn't want to be bothered with sex and all that sort of thing.**

SOMERSET MAUGHAM

The summer of 1839 was a season of simmering, suppressed passion for a young woman named Florence Nightingale. With voices inside her head already hinting at her future calling as the lady of the lamp and ten-pound note, she had decided she would never marry. However, when her cousin Henry Nicholson fell in love with her, she encouraged him in his advances, because being near to him meant she could also be near to the true object of her desires, Henry's sister Marianne. 'I never loved but one person with passion in my life and that was her,' Florence wrote some years later. After that first summer, the lives of Florence, Henry and Marianne stayed locked in an unrequited triangle for four years, until Henry finally proposed marriage. When Florence turned him down, Marianne was so upset on her brother's account that she severed all ties with the Nightingale family. Florence was devastated. Her misery was only relieved when she turned her thoughts to those suffering more than herself . . .

" **This is the nature of women, not to love when we love them, and to love when we love them not.**

CERVANTES

Not declaring your true feelings to the love of your life may preserve an impossible dream for a little longer, but it can also affect your hold on reality. When filming *The Millionairess*, Peter Sellers fell madly in love with his co-star Sophia Loren, and told all his friends (including his wife) about it . . . but not once did he seriously question whether Sophia felt the same way. The film's producer had noticed that from the moment they met Sellers treated her as if she was the Queen of England. She, on the other hand, was simply 'nice to him'. When, for a later film, it was suggested that Sellers might again be her co-star, Ms Loren rejected the idea out of hand. Her autobiography, published in 1976, did nothing for Sellers' pride; he wasn't even mentioned. Sellers, obviously disappointed, tried to shrug it off by pointing out that he hadn't got a mention in the Bible either.

Like many girls before and since, Lulu had a teenage crush on a hunky male pop star (or two). Her feelings for the sixties heart-throb Scott Walker swung from the distant adoration of a fan to unrequited, exquisite agony when she met him in the flesh and actually worked with him. She was just fifteen when she met another hero, guitarist Eric Clapton. Again her wild Celtic heart pounded, but again the infatuation was only one-way. Paul McCartney, aware of her crush on Clapton, would tease her for years afterwards by asking, each time they met, 'How's Eric?'

For the Beatles' manager Brian Epstein, promoting the band was a labour of love. After being 'crazy about him for ages', he finally got round to kissing John Lennon. Lennon did not deny they had kissed, but discounted the idea that they had actually had an affair. As he said, shortly before his death in 1980, 'It was never consummated.'

**Never get into a narrow double bed with a wide single man.**

QUENTIN CRISP

Salvador Dali, painter of such works as *The Spectre of Sex Appeal*, *Soft Self-Portrait with Grilled Bacon* and *The Great Masturbator*, was the object of unrequited passion for the great Spanish poet, Fédérico Garcia Lorca. 'He was homosexual, as everyone knows, and madly in love with me,' Dali claimed. When Lorca made advances towards him, Dali expressed annoyance, since he wasn't a homosexual himself. Nor was he about to become one for Lorca's benefit; in Dali's words, 'it hurts'. Still, looking back, he admitted there was something very flattering about being seduced (almost) by such a fine poet and he did wonder if he'd been wrong to deny Lorca 'a tiny bit of the Divine Dali's asshole'.

Norman Parkinson, having photographed so many of the world's most beautiful women, stunned a gathering of pressmen with the confession that of all the females he had viewed through the camera lens, the one with the most sex appeal was Margaret Thatcher. Writing in the *Sunday Telegraph* about Mrs Thatcher and the 'aphrodisiac pull of power', Selina Hastings told how 'for the armed forces she is far and away the favourite object of sexual fantasy'. If the Thatchers ever split up, Parkinson would be up against some stiff competition in the battle for her affections.

Alfred Hitchcock spent a great deal of his working life looking at attractive blondes through a camera lens. And if they had any sense that was as close as they allowed him to get. According to Kenneth Anger's *Hollywood Babylon II*, Grace Kelly performed a special one-off favour for the drooling director by undressing at her bedroom window, with the curtains open and the light on. The view from Hitchcock's 'Rear Window' a mile away was enhanced by a powerful telescope. In later years, Hitch liked to refer to her as 'Princess Disgrace'.

" **A woman should be like a good suspense film; the more left to the imagination the more excitement there is.**

ALFRED HITCHCOCK

" **I am fond of children (except boys).**

LEWIS CARROLL

Eminent researchers have tried their hardest to dig up some dirt with regard to The Reverend Charles Dodgson, a.k.a. Lewis Carroll, and his fondness for little girls like Alice Liddell, the original Alice in Wonderland, but evidence is scarce. Whilst he did confess to having 'unholy thoughts, which torture with their hateful presence the fancy that would fain be pure', it is unlikely that the Reverend gave them any fuller expression. At thirty-three he revealed the extent of his fondness for the actress Ellen Terry, then just seventeen: 'I can imagine no more delightful occupation than brushing Ellen Terry's hair!'

Ellen Terry's 'affair by post' with Bernard Shaw was so agreeable to both parties that they feared ever meeting, in case it ruined everything. Once, when she entered a room and heard Shaw's voice, she immediately turned and fled. 'I think I'd rather not meet you – in the flesh,' she wrote. 'I, too, fear to break the spell,' wrote Shaw. 'Remorses, presentiments, all sorts of tendernesses wring my heart at the thought of materializing this beautiful friendship of ours by a meeting.' Ellen's passion increased: 'I love you more every minute. I can't help it, and I guessed it would be like that! And so we won't meet.' In the end they did meet but, keeping their hands off each other, they kept the relationship intact.

For some, Hans Christian Andersen, writer of so many classic fairy-tales, was a bit of a fairy himself. However there is no denying that he carried a torch for the opera star Jenny

Lind, also known as 'The Swedish Nightingale'. They first met in 1840 in Copenhagen, a purely formal meeting between two celebrities of the day. Then, in 1843, Andersen saw her performing. 'In love' was the simple entry for his diary on that day. A week later he had not got over it; 'I love her' he wrote. At the time Andersen was 38 and Jenny Lind just 23, but since they were both successful in their chosen arts, they found plenty to talk about and got on well. However, at an early stage Jenny had to admit she did not love him. Over two years of letter-writing, Andersen kept hoping that she would change her mind, but from Jenny the message was always the same. Then they met again at a dinner. Andersen's diary entry 'She toasted me as her brother!' marks his dejected acceptance that their relationship could never be more than platonic. But he never lost his admiration for her and his tale *The Nightingale* is a tribute to the girl that got away.

> **Women are like elephants to me; I like to look at them but I wouldn't want to own one.**
>
> W. C. FIELDS

The most carefully planned platonic, brother/sister relationships can sometimes end in failure, i.e. marriage. In February 1924, Enid Blyton and her editor, Hugh Pollock, realized that something was going on between them and did their best to keep it under control. 'We're going to try and be real friends and not fall in love!' she wrote in her diary, and the next day she outlined their plans for 'a purely platonic friendship'. After three months they would see how things stood. 'Oh dear,' wrote Enid. Then, in a letter, Hugh told her he was fond of her 'in a big brotherly sort of way'. Enid's response? 'I'll small sister him.' Clearly three months was too long for her to wait. The next day she wrote him 'a long letter telling him exactly what I think. Guess he won't like it much, but he's going to fall in love if he hasn't already. I want him for mine.' A little less than six months later, they were married.

Casanova never married, but he once came dangerously close. What was it about the seventeen-year-old beauty Leonilda that made the middle-aged libertine even consider this drastic step? Perhaps there was a touch of vanity in the attraction, as Casanova saw in her features a passing resemblance to himself. It was only when he met the girl's mother that he realized the truth. The girl was his daughter, the outcome of a liaison seventeen years and nine months earlier!

Casanova and Leonilda had a good reason for keeping their relationship on the platonic level, but Edward the Confessor may not have been so readily convinced when, on his wedding night, his wife Editha refused to make love. She claimed she was only playing impossible to get for *his* benefit. What better test could there be of his ability to resist temptation? Somewhat flummoxed, Edward shrugged and channelled his energies into building Westminster Abbey instead.

Both Princess Margaret and Peter Townsend were keen to marry after Townsend's divorce in 1952. At the Queen's coronation the next year it was clear that the two were in love; the way Margaret picked a piece of fluff off his sleeve was an unthinking but undeniable show of affection, witnessed by millions of television viewers. But the Church's views on divorce made speculation about their possible marriage a source of some embarrassment and Townsend was soon posted abroad. In October 1953, after plenty of behind-the-scenes squabbling between pro and anti factions, Margaret made a statement to the press: 'I would like it to be known that I have decided not to marry Group Captain Peter Townsend. I have been aware that, subject to renouncing my rights of succession, it might have been possible for me to contract a civil marriage. But, mindful of the Church's teachings that Christian marriage is indissoluble, I have resolved to put these considerations before all others.' In 1960 she married Tony Armstrong-Jones but, as the world knows, the marriage has since been dissolved.

For William Pitt the Younger, it was not a consideration of state but a family illness that prevented him for marrying his Even Younger companion, Eleanor Eden. As their relationship proceeded, with no formal announcement of an engagement, the couple became easy targets for gossips and the newspapers. Eleanor was keen on marriage, but in the end Pitt had to reveal that it would never happen. Both he and his father were prone to moments of sudden madness, rushes of blood which Pitt himself described as 'a tumult, a heat in the brain'. With it could come genius, but also a terrible rage. On one occasion, when a gang attacked his carriage, he had almost strangled one of the attackers and it had taken four friends to pull him off. So as not to pass on this frightening instability, William had promised his father on his deathbed that he would never have children. He kept his word and the illness died with him, some six years after his separation from Eleanor.

As far as Ernest Hemingway was concerned, the only thing that prevented him from having an affair with Marlene Dietrich was bad timing. Or, as he put it, they were 'victims of unsynchronized passion'. He claimed they had been in love since their first meeting, but they had never slept together, because whenever he was free, she would be deeply in love with someone else and, similarly, whenever she was free, 'on the surface and swimming about, with those marvellously seeking eyes of hers', Hemingway was 'submerged'.

## BEYOND REACH

All kinds of barriers can stand between a couple and living happily ever after. But bad timing, family madness, the obligations of royalty, and even Casanova's incestuous complications are all minor hurdles in comparison to the one that separated the former dictator of Uganda, Idi Amin, and President Nyerere of Tanzania. In 1972, Amin wrote to Nyerere: 'With these few words I want to assure you that I love you and if you had been a woman I would have considered marrying you, although your head is full of grey hairs, but as you are a man that possibility doesn't arise . . .'

# CHAPTER EIGHT

# TYING THE KNOT

## The big decision, the big day

*Why was David Bowie late for his wedding? What happened to Archbishop Desmond Tutu's trousers? What did Churchill do in the church? How did Enid Blyton feel about it all? And why get married anyway?*

> **A man and a woman marry because both of them don't know what to do with themselves.**
>
> ANTON CHEKHOV

Some marry for love, some for money; William Shakespeare and Charlie Chaplin had more pressing reasons, having got their girls 'into trouble'; Ella Fitzgerald was even crazy enough to get married for a bet; Charles Darwin, on the other hand, adopted a more scientific approach . . .

Darwin was thirty-six and yet to reach his conclusions on *The Origin of the Species* when he made his assessment of the pros and cons of marriage by drawing up two columns in his notebook, headed 'MARRY' and 'NOT MARRY'.

The advantages of marriage included: children ('if it please God'), having a constant companion, a friend who would be interested in him . . . an 'object to be beloved and played with – better than a dog, anyhow'; 'Home, and someone to take care of the house – charms of music and female chit-chat. These things good for one's health.'

Disadvantages included: 'the expense and anxiety of children . . . loss of time . . . cannot read in the evenings . . . fatness and idleness . . . if any children, forced to gain one's bread.'

By the end of his notes, he had decided that marriage was a less daunting prospect than that of facing old age alone. Beneath the scribbled words 'Marry – Marry – Marry', he wrote 'QED' as if he had just proved a scientific theorem. Six months later, he proposed to his cousin Emma Wedgwood (granddaughter of Josiah) and, to his surprise, was accepted on the spot. Only then did he come to realize another drawback: 'I wish the awful day was over,' he wrote to her, in dread of all the fuss and attention the actual wedding would involve. Still, once it *was* over, he had few regrets about his momentous decision. 'I marvel at my good fortune,' he wrote in his autobiography, years later, 'that she, so infinitely my superior in every single moral quality, consented to be my wife.'

> **By all means marry. If you get a good wife you'll become happy; if you get a bad one you'll become a philosopher.**
> SOCRATES

'Bet you wouldn't marry me!' At twenty years old Ella Fitzgerald was already on her way to becoming the first lady of jazz and certainly didn't need to resort to such a desperate gamble for a bit of cash. But when a very casual acquaintance jokingly made the remark, Ella – for the hell of it – decided to prove him wrong. Within hours they were man and wife. The rest of Ella's band were flabbergasted and bandleader Chick Webb, who was also acting as her guardian, insisted the marriage be annulled. In court, the judge was stern, but sympathetic. 'You just keep singing "A-Tisket A-Tasket",' he told her (the song was Number One in the US hit parade), 'and leave those men alone.' In an interview several years later, Ella admitted that getting married for a bet was one of the stupidest things she'd ever done. She also had trouble remembering her first husband's name.

**❝ There's one fool at least in every married couple.**

HENRY FIELDING

Lillie Langtry is best known for the long-running affair she enjoyed with Edward VII, before he became king and she made a name for herself on the stage. Her reason for marrying

Mr Edward Langtry, besides the alliterative potential his sur-
name offered to Lillie the aspiring actress, was his wealth. She
particularly liked the look of his yacht. Years later she would
remark, 'To become the mistress of the yacht, I married the
owner.'

> **I haven't heard of girls being attracted
> by *poor* old men.**
>
> SOPHIA LOREN

When Grace Kelly became engaged to Prince Rainier of
Monaco, Marilyn Monroe congratulated her warmly, but also
recognized the practical implications of the match. 'I'm so glad
you've found a way out of this business,' she told her.

Money was the main reason for George IV entering into one
of royalty's most disastrous marriages, to Caroline of
Brunswick. His heavy drinking and even heavier gambling
debts had left him owing more than £600,000 (which today
would be several millions). William Pitt's government could
only be talked into paying off these debts on condition that
George married and produced an heir. In spite of the financial
incentive, it was only a last-ditch intervention by his father,
George III, that stopped him escaping from the church. And,
thanks to the groom's extremely good friend Lady Jersey, the
bride had more than the usual butterflies in her stomach; with
George's amused approval, his jealous mistress had laced
Caroline's breakfast with Epsom salts.

Alec Guinness's wedding day was not without its moments
of comedy. Before getting to the Register Office, he was
congratulated by an old actor friend and, as a result of shaking
hands over the rose-bush that stood between them, they both

ended up with scratches from the thorns. Besides a slight problem with keeping hold of his top hat in his nervous and bloody fingers, the journey to the Reigate Register Office passed reasonably smoothly. It was only on arriving there that Guinness realized he had forgotten the money to pay for the marriage licence. In the best Ealing Film tradition, his friendly London cabbie came to the rescue and lent him the necessary few quid. 'Best of luck to yer, guv!'

> **All tragedies are finished by a death,**
> **All comedies are ended by a marriage.**
>
> LORD BYRON

Everyone involved in a wedding hopes the sun will shine, but Spike Milligan and his third wife Shelagh had too much of a good thing when they married on a scorching July day. It was so hot inside the church, that Spike climbed up onto a pew and removed part of the roof to let some air in!

*And now, a Goon Show script that got away . . .*

## . . . THE TALE OF THE GROOM'S MISSING TROUSERS

Archbishop Desmond Tutu was a far from wealthy man when he got married in July 1955. As he was in need of a new suit for the ceremony, his sister Sylvia offered to buy him one as a wedding present. When the big day arrived, Sylvia and the new suit had still not materialized. With the minutes ticking away, an underpanted, underdressed Desmond Tutu started eyeing his only other suit, which his best man had borrowed for the day. Happily, before proceedings could sink to the level of a Whitehall farce, Sylvia turned up with the new suit and the best man was allowed to keep his trousers on.

If it is not the groom's suit, it is usually the bride who arrives a little late. However, on 9 March 1796, Josephine was left fretting at the registrar's office for a good two hours before her husband-to-be turned up. Napoleon was a busy man. So busy in fact, that their honeymoon only lasted one day (and night) before he dashed off again to war.

Rock Hudson and Phyllis Gates travelled together to their wedding, but found themselves behind schedule after meeting some friends at the airport and then stopping off to pick up their marriage licence. They were racing on to the ceremony itself when the procession was halted by a speed-cop, who presented the groom with a $27 ticket. But that was cheap compared to the $35,000 house, Ford Thunderbird and $250 a week that Hudson had to cough up after the divorce.

Margaret Thatcher dressed rather more conservatively on the day she married Denis at Wesley's Chapel in the City of London in 1951. It was a freezing, foggy December day, which is why the bride's sapphire blue dress was made of velvet. Beneath her matching hat and grey ostrich feather, she was determined to keep warm on her last day as Miss Roberts. With her renowned practicality, she used the dress for evening wear for some time afterwards. 'It's probably still in the attic somewhere . . .'

> **A man who got married in order to be a better Prime Minister wouldn't be either a good Prime Minister or a good husband.**
>
> EDWARD HEATH

When Vladimir Ilyich Ulyanov (better known as Lenin) married his fellow revolutionary Krupskaya, he was surprised when the priest refused to conduct the service unless the bride was given a ring. Fortunately one of Lenin's friends happened to be an apprentice jeweller, and he swiftly fashioned two rings for the young couple from a melted down five-copeck piece. The Lenins then set up home, with Krupskaya's mother under the same roof. Many years later, as the most powerful man in Russia, he was asked what the heaviest punishment for bigamy should be. With a smile, he replied, 'having two mothers-in-law'.

> **I find lovemaking a serious and delightful occupation.**
>
> WINSTON CHURCHILL

As soon as his wedding ceremony was over, Winston Churchill is said to have discussed affairs of state with David Lloyd George in the vestry, leaving his newly-wedded wife, Clemmie, to chat with their bemused friends and relations. He also kept busy during their honeymoon, breaking off from the 'serious and delightful occupation' of lovemaking to write his book *My African Journey*.

For Joan Rivers, her first marriage was chiefly a matter of doing what her parents expected of her. Knowing in her heart that something was wrong, she took a tranquillizer to see her through the ceremony. The rabbi conducting the service must have sensed a need to liven things up, as he managed to drag the sleeve of his gown through the flame of a ceremonial candle, setting himself on fire. As Joan feared, there was nothing else to set the relationship alight and, after six months of fights and marriage counselling, they separated.

Robinson

> **If women are to effect a significant amelioration in their condition, it seems obvious that they must refuse to marry.**
> GERMAINE GREER, *The Female Eunuch*

Nowadays it's up to the bride to choose whether she wants to 'love and honour' or 'love, honour and obey'. 'Love, honour and feed' is a less accepted variation, suggested by Barbra Streisand when she married actor Elliot Gould in 1963, on the grounds that there are few things more important than making sure a person is well fed.

> **I always feel you are as old as you think or feel you are. I think Diana will keep me young. That's a very good thing. I shall be exhausted.**
>
> PRINCE CHARLES

On 29 July 1981, Lady Diana Spencer was another to take an idiosyncratic approach to the marriage vows, juggling with her husband's Christian names and marrying herself to 'Philip Charles' rather than 'Charles Philip'. What caused the slip? Had her mind suddenly leapt back to the announcement of their engagement in February, when Britain's biggest selling communist paper, the *Morning Star*, had warned her of what the future would hold? . . .

## DON'T DO IT DIANA

> Lady Diana Spencer is to sacrifice her independence to a domineering layabout for the sake of a few lousy foreign holidays. As the future Queen of England she can expect a fair bit of first class travel and a lot of attention, but with a £100,000 home of her own and a steady job as an exclusive nursery nurse, who needs it?

## DON'T DO IT CHARLIE

No, it's not another headline from the *Morning Star*, but the command of Mick Jagger to fellow Rolling Stone Charlie Watts, when the taciturn drummer announced his plans to marry his girlfriend, Shirley. That was in 1964, when the Stones were capitalizing on the rebellious contrast they offered to the cosy 'boy-next-door' image of the Beatles. A Stone getting married could seriously jeopardize record sales. That October, after much bickering within the band, Charlie and

Shirley married in secret. Jagger's attitude to marriage had softened by 1971, when he married Bianca. Some friends even reported that during his earlier affair with Marianne Faithfull, he had proposed marriage but that she, more rebellious than the 'rebel', had refused.

In Mozart's opera *The Marriage of Figaro*, Figaro is obliged by a contract to marry a woman he does not desire. In real life, Mozart himself had signed a contract committing himself to a woman he *did* desire. Constanze Weber's mother and her guardian were both aware of Mozart's talent and eligibility, and were also anxious to preserve Constanze's reputation. Mozart's father Leopold was against the match, and it took a lot of pleading from Wolfgang to obtain his grudging consent, which arrived by letter on the day after the wedding. According to Mozart, the ceremony itself was so moving that everyone, including the priest, wept with joy. Presumably even the wedding cake was in tiers . . .

> " **A bachelor, in my opinion, is only half alive.**
>
> MOZART

'Is it better to get married or remain a bachelor?' The question was put to Franz Liszt by a member of the audience at one of his piano recitals. Liszt encouraged this sort of participation, inviting concert-goers to put written requests into a box at the hall entrance. Originally, people would simply ask him to improvise on well-known pieces, but soon more abstract themes were offered as inspiration, including the vexed question of marriage. Before laying a finger on his keyboard, Liszt (who never married, despite countless liaisons and two long-running affairs) informed his audience that 'whatever decision one makes about marrying or remaining single, one will live to regret it'.

66 **Every woman should marry — and no man.**

BENJAMIN DISRAELI

Pablo Picasso had no regrets about being single, having lived quite contentedly 'in sin' with successive lovers, until he met the Russian ballerina Olga Koklova. Unlike most of the women in Picasso's experience, she showed no signs of warming to his charm and would lock him out of her hotel room, insisting that he never come in. Of course this only aroused Picasso's curiosity. The great impresario Diaghilev warned him to be careful. 'You have to marry Russian girls,' he told him. Picasso merely laughed. 'You must be joking!' he said. One year later, Olga became the first Mrs Picasso.

66 **When I am married, I want to be single, and when I am single, I want to be married.**

CARY GRANT

The magazine *Punch* had some blunt advice for those about to marry: 'Don't.' Enid Blyton, in an article on humour for *Teacher's World* magazine, described this advice as 'very silly'. On her second wedding anniversary in August 1926 she wrote in her diary: 'I *am* glad I married Hugh and I wouldn't be unmarried for worlds. He is such a perfect dear.' However, after a further fifteen years, the marriage was showing signs of wear. In 1941, on a spring evening in Budleigh Salterton, she met the tanned handsome doctor who was to become her second husband.

Karl Marx's doubts about marriage were partly founded on the hard times he had put his wife Jenny through. He didn't want to see his daughter Laura suffer for *her* husband's labours. In a letter to one of Laura's suitors, Marx wrote: 'You know that I have sacrificed my whole fortune to the revolutionary struggle. I do not regret it. Quite the contrary. If I had to start my life again, I would do the same. But I would not marry.'

Few men walked more reluctantly down the aisle than Henry VIII for his marriage to Anne of Cleves. As he confided to his minister Thomas Cromwell shortly before the ceremony: 'If it were not to satisfy the world and my realm, I would not do what I must do this day for none earthly thing.' Within seven months they were divorced.

66 **Marriage is rather a silly habit.**

JOHN OSBORNE

'Doomed from the start.' That's how Richard Burton described his second marriage to Liz Taylor. The ceremony took place in the unlikely setting of the Botswana bushlands, conducted by a District Commissioner of the local Tswana tribe. Ominously, Burton contracted malaria whilst on the trip. He recovered, but the marriage lasted less than a year.

The 'doomed' marriage of all time was the one between Adolf Hitler and Eva Braun. In the early hours of Sunday 29 April 1945, the ceremony in Hitler's Berlin bunker was witnessed by Paul Josef Goebbels, his Minister of Public Enlightenment and Propaganda, and Martin Bormann. Previously Hitler had rejected the possibility of ever getting married, on the grounds that it would hold back his career. But now there wasn't much career left to hold back. Little more than twenty-four hours after the ceremony, the newlyweds said farewell to their friends and retired to Hitler's suite, where Eva took poison and her husband shot himself in the head.

Mahatma Gandhi's marriage was rather different. At the age of thirteen, in a thrifty triple wedding for himself, his brother and his cousin, Gandhi entered into an arranged marriage with a young girl called Kasturbai. She was not impressed with the young teenager's attempts at being a domineering husband. 'I learnt the lesson of non-violence from my wife when I tried to bend her to my will,' said Gandhi. 'Her determined resistance to my will . . . and her quiet submission to the suffering my stupidity involved . . . ultimately made me ashamed of myself and cured me of my stupidity in thinking that I was born to rule over her; and in the end she became my teacher in non-violence.' Their marriage lasted a little longer than Mr and Mrs Hitler's – sixty-two years.

Charlie Chaplin married his second wife, fifteen-year-old Lita Grey, because she was pregnant and it was the only way he could get out of standing trial for having sex with a minor. At the wedding party, he told his friends: 'Well, boys, this is better than the penitentiary, but it won't last.' He was right – two years later his young wife filed for divorce.

The wedding reception offers the chance for all to relax, congratulate the happy couple and lay into the food and drink. Condolences are not usually in order. However, when George Orwell married his first wife Eileen O'Shaughnessy, he had already gone down the Road to Wigan Pier and was showing all the characteristics of a restless, but determined artist. At the pub wedding reception, Orwell's mother and sister took his young bride upstairs and offered her their sincere sympathy: George was not going to be easy to live with. Eileen assured them she knew what she was letting herself in for. But not even she could have foreseen that within a year she'd be caught up in the Spanish Civil War, by George's side in the fight against the Fascists.

Q: In what way was George Harrison's wedding different from that of his fellow Beatles?

A: *George had been more careful. John, Paul and Ringo were all expectant fathers when they first tied the knot.*

Still, they were in illustrious company. Back in 1582, an eighteen-year-old tearaway called William Shakespeare had his way with young Anne Hathaway. Baby Susanna was born in May 1583, six months after her parents' November wedding. To the immense frustration of Shakespearian enthusiasts, the register which the couple signed was later thrown on to a fire to help boil the curate's kettle.

Nat King Cole got so drunk on his stag night, that his fiancée Maria barely spoke to him the next day, the eve of their wedding. Then, at the reception, Nat again got a 'wee bit smashed'. And so, the morning after, instead of nursing fond memories of their first night as husband and wife, Nat was nursing a hangover and his memory was a complete blank.

Roger Moore was enjoying fame as 'The Saint', when he at last secured a divorce from his second wife Dorothy Squires in order to marry Luisa, the woman with whom he had been living for eight years. At the reception, when Roger was asked by a journalist if this, his third wedding, would also be his last, Luisa picked up a knife and said 'I'll kill him if it's not!'

16 August 1985 was Madonna's twenty-sixth birthday and the date of her wedding to Sean Penn. They had tried to keep the clifftop location in Malibu a secret from the world's press, but someone must have squealed, because before the bowler-hatted Madonna could say 'I do', a fleet of helicopters hummed into view, paparazzi snapping away from every cockpit. Mr and Mrs Penn continued with the festivities as best they could and offered a cheerful foretaste of what was to come, when they pushed slices of the wedding cake into each other's faces.

The wedding cake held a deeper significance for Nelson and Winnie Mandela. In June 1958 they were due to marry in two separate ceremonies, one at Winnie's parents' home, the other at Nelson's. But due to his political commitments and impending trial for treason, there was no time for the second ceremony. The half of the wedding cake which was to be eaten at Nelson's home was left intact and stored away in Winnie's home, not to be eaten until Nelson's release . . .

# CHAPTER NINE

# HOW WAS IT FOR YOU?

*Honeymoon highlights, first-night flops and other intimate moments*

*T*chaikovsky didn't want to start, Victor Hugo couldn't stop! The press watched John and Yoko, Halley watched his comet; Mickey Rooney took his golf clubs, Nancy Reagan took her parents . . . Honeymoons vary so greatly in their highs and lows, and even in the range of activities, that there is only one thing they all have in common. Elizabeth Taylor's second husband, actor Michael Wilding, put his finger on it when asked how he and his young bride were going to spend their honeymoon. His reply? 'Together.'

*B*rian Rix has made more money with his trousers round his ankles than all but the most exclusive gigolos. He and his wife, Elspet Gray, spent their wedding night at the perfect honeymoon location for the king of saucy Whitehall farce – a charming English hostelry called 'The Cock Inn'.

*T*here was a right cock-up when Dr David Owen and his American wife Debbie checked into their New York hotel for their wedding night on 28 December 1978. Naturally they had booked in advance, but the hotel had failed to reserve the appropriate room. In the end the far-from-happy couple were offered a room which Owen could only describe as 'sordid'. They were about to leave the hotel to look elsewhere, when a member of the staff saw their wedding photo in an early edition of the *New York Times*. Since the caption mentioned that the groom was British Minister for the Navy, the hotel staff immediately offered the Owens the Bridal Suite. Unimpressed by the hotel's double standards, David and Debbie stormed out. They ended up staying at a friend's flat, where they were obliged to share a single bed – cramped but cosy!

> **The Americans, like the English, probably make love worse than any other race.**
>
> WALT WHITMAN
> (*How did he know?*)

Walt and Lillian Disney were married on 13 July 1925. Lillian deserves a particular place in history for telling her husband that Mortimer (Walt's choice) was a 'sissy' name for a mouse and Mickey would be much better. Their first night as man and wife was spent on a train bound for Seattle, from where they were due to embark on a special honeymoon cruise. However, before they could slip into their pyjamas, Walt felt the first pangs of a vicious toothache. Leaving Lillian to sleep on her own, Walt spent his wedding night with the train's porter, polishing passengers' shoes, which he said helped him take his mind off the pain. The offending tooth was yanked out by a dentist in Seattle. Walt needed a few days recuperation, but after that the Disneys were at last able to commence their cruise . . . among other things.

" **The success of the marriage comes after the failure of the honeymoon.**

G. K. CHESTERTON

The Queen Mother had an uncomfortable honeymoon, being laid low with a bout of whooping cough. And the Queen of Crimewriters, Agatha Christie, was not in the best of health after a few days on honeymoon with her second husband Max, an archaeologist fifteen years her junior. Not the types to spend a fortnight lounging around in bed, they set out on an active holiday through Italy, Yugoslavia and Greece, walking mile upon mile over rough terrain, mountains and rivers, and occasionally 'taking it easy' by trekking on mules. There can be no doubt that Agatha, just turned forty, found it a struggle to keep up with her twenty-five-year-old husband. In her diary, she made an unusual entry for a honeymooner: 'Acute feeling of misery and indeed regret that I had ever married Max – He's too young for me!!' By the end of the day, though, he was just about forgiven: 'Arrived nearer dead than alive – Max ministered to me so well that I am glad I married him after all. But he mustn't do it again!!'

Another active honeymooner was Mickey Rooney. You'd have thought he'd have had his hands full with the voluptuous actress Ava Gardner, but he clearly missed the point when told that the object of a honeymoon is to play around. Why else should he take his golf clubs with him?

Ronald and Nancy Reagan were far too sociable to spend their honeymoon alone; Nancy's mum and dad also came along for the ride. 'Having a honeymoon with your parents may seem strange to some people,' said Nancy, 'but somehow it seemed perfectly natural to us.'

A more romantic picture is that of young lovers gazing up at a star-filled sky, without parental supervision. However, even a clear, starry night can lose its magic if you are on honeymoon with an astronomer. Instead of admiring his new wife's heavenly body, Edmund Halley left her in bed, while he went out to watch the comet that now bears his name.

> **Seeing the Niagara Falls after the first night of the honeymoon must have been the bride's second greatest disappointment.**
>
> OSCAR WILDE

Robert Graves and his wife Nancy also spent part of their wedding night looking up at the sky. As Graves recounts in his memoirs of the First World War *Goodbye to All That*, both he and Nancy were rather inexperienced and the sexual side of things was not going too smoothly, when suddenly the earth moved – literally. A German bomb had landed nearby. After the clumsy embarrassment of the previous hour, it came as something of a relief to be interrupted by an air raid.

During the Second World War, it was not a bomb that interrupted the extremely famous James Cagney and not-quite-so-famous Merle Oberon, as they cavorted beneath the sheets. 'Just imagine,' Merle suddenly exclaimed, 'I'm in bed with Jimmy Cagney!' Mr Cagney was not so thrilled, and resumed the proceedings with noticeably less intensity.

Napoleon and Josephine were busy consummating their marriage when Napoleon suddenly cried out, not in ecstasy but in agony. His leg had just been bitten by Josephine's poodle, a jealous pet named Fortuné. With time for only one night of honeymoon before returning to the battlefront, Napoleon put his foot down (albeit gingerly): 'Either the dog goes or I go.' Josephine, stroking the yapping Fortuné, bade her husband farewell. The stunned Napoleon swiftly backed down and, climbing carefully into bed, resigned himself to a *ménagerie à trois*.

It used to be the tradition on a royal wedding night for the couple to enter the nuptial bed with the court in attendance. When William of Orange and his new wife, Mary, climbed in, King Charles II personally closed the curtains round the bed and shouted encouragement from the touchline. 'Now, nephew, to your work,' he cried, 'Hey! St George for England!'

Fifty reporters and photographers crammed eagerly into one hotel bedroom when John Lennon and Yoko Ono started their honeymoon in March 1969. The bride and groom had announced that a 'happening' was going to take place, which, for the world's press, could mean only one thing. 'These guys were sweating to fight to get in first,' John Lennon later recalled, 'because they thought we were going to be making love in bed.' Since John and Yoko had already appeared in full frontal poses on the cover of their *Two Virgins* LP, it must have come as something of a shock to see them sitting up in bed, wearing pyjamas. 'I hope it's not a let-down,' John told them. 'We wouldn't make love in public – that's an emotionally personal thing.' Their 'bed-in', a protest against the suffering and violence in the world, went on for one, sex-free, week.

Another pair of musical honeymooners in 1969 were Lulu and Maurice Gibb, the bearded Bee Gee. Their planned trip to Acapulco had to wait until after the Eurovision song contest, for which Lulu sang a romantic little number called 'Boom Bang-a-Bang'.

There was a four-week delay before Charles Kingsley, author of *The Water Babies*, and his wife Fanny consummated their marriage. They didn't want to rush into things. Although the Victorian Era may appear to have been a time of widespread sexual hypocrisy, here at least were two young people who *had* been sheltered from the horrors of the flesh. Charles expressed his trepidation in a letter to Fanny shortly before their marriage. 'I have been thinking over your terror at seeing me undressed and I feel that I should have the same feeling in a minor degree to you, till I had learnt to bear the blaze of your naked beauty. You do not know how often a man is struck powerless in body and mind on his wedding night.' So hesitant were they about this mutual terror that they did not make love until their honeymoon was in its fifth and final week; for the next seven days, on the rare occasions when they were spotted, they were both beaming broadly.

Still, better late than never. The girl now known as Saint Cecilia, patron saint of music and musicians, had some bad news for her husband on their wedding night. Her body, she told him, was guarded by an angel, to whom she had already pledged herself. Whoever the guardian angel was, it had its work cut out when a commission of priests sentenced Cecilia to death for her beliefs. The angel managed to save her from her first attempted execution, suffocation in a deliberately overheated bathroom, by causing a failure in the heating system. But sadly for the singing saint, not even an angel could save her from decapitation.

## HOW WAS IT FOR YOU?

Rudolph Valentino's first marriage, to a little-known actress named Jean Acker, could not have got off to a worse start. On their wedding night, the silver screen's 'Great Lover' was about to pick up his new wife and carry her over the threshold of the bridal suite, when she leapt out of his reach and into the room, locking the door behind her. At first he took it as a joke, but his knocking on the door grew increasingly frenetic when Mrs Valentino, calling from the other side, told him she was having second thoughts about the marriage. She never did let him in.

66 **I thought of losing my virginity as a career move.**

**MADONNA**

In the 1933 film *The Private Life Of Henry VIII*, starring Charles Laughton, Henry and his fourth wife, Anne of Cleves, are shown playing cards on their wedding night. By all accounts, they never got up to anything more exciting in bed. 'When he comes to bed he kisseth me,' said Anne, 'and taketh me by the hand and biddeth me "goodnight, sweetheart" – and in the morning kisseth me and biddeth me "farewell, darling"'. Henry, in his private papers, confirmed that he left her 'as good a maid' as he found her.

It was a miracle that George IV and his wife Caroline of Brunswick ever consummated their marriage, since neither found the other at all attractive and George had anaesthetized himself with booze to see him through the wedding night. Still, they managed it somehow. Then, duty done, George staggered out of bed and into the fireplace, where he spent the rest of the night in a drunken stupor.

A second miracle in the love-life of George and Caroline is the biological accomplishment that they share with two other famous couples – Victor 'Nine-Times-A-Night' Hugo and his wife Adèle, and Elvis and Priscilla Presley . . .

All three of the ladies involved gave birth to a child *exactly* nine months after their wedding night. When Queen Caroline was told she was pregnant, she gave a derisive laugh and said, 'I don't believe it!' Adèle Hugo must have been less surprised; on their wedding night – and most other nights . . . and most mornings . . . and afternoons – Monsieur Hugo just couldn't get enough. If Caroline's pregnancy was a miracle, Adèle's was proof of the Laws of Probability.

For Elvis and Priscilla it was more a case of 'practice makes perfect'. They slept together for hundreds of nights without making love, as Elvis was determined to make it a 'special' occasion. That occasion turned out to be their wedding night. Before then, they contented themselves with fantasy games on Elvis's king-sized bed at Graceland. Polaroid and video technology had just become available, so Priscilla was soon appearing on film as schoolgirl, teacher or secretary under Elvis's skilled direction. The most embarrassing thing for Priscilla was sneaking out at all hours to make bulk purchases of film. Her face became so familiar at the local chemists that she started trying to justify the orders, by saying her pictures weren't coming out properly or someone had stolen her film. Their wedding day and 'special' night finally came on 1 May 1967. After the long, long wait, Priscilla was not disappointed. According to her, 'he made it special, like he did with anything he took pride in'.

> **I found I liked sexual intercourse
> because of its amazing power of
> producing a celestial flood of emotion
> and exaltation of existence.**
>
> GEORGE BERNARD SHAW

It was not so special for the writer Virginia Woolf, who was thirty when she married Leonard Woolf. She clearly did not feel she had missed out by keeping her virginity through her twenties. 'Why do you think people make such a fuss about marriage and copulation?' she wrote to her friend Vanessa Bell, whilst still away on her honeymoon. 'Why do some of our friends change upon losing chastity? Possibly my great age makes it less of a catastrophe; but certainly I find the climax immensely exaggerated.'

Martina Navratilova thought much the same after her first sexual experience. 'There were no bells, no stars, no flashing lights . . . and not a lot of affection or skill either.' Seventeen-year-old Martina and her boyfriend had made the most of his parents' Prague apartment, while the parents were away for the weekend. Besides finding it all a bit painful, Martina was further racked with worry when her next period failed to start on time. She is certainly not the only female in history to have made the mistake of leaving the question of birth control entirely to her male partner. Wimbledon nearly lost a great champion – the days passed, with Martina agonizing over the choice of having an abortion or sacrificing her tennis career, before her period made its belated but welcome appearance. Incidentally, the gentleman involved is now married with, at the latest count, four children.

Whilst Herbert Henry Asquith was working his way up to the post of Prime Minister of Britain, his wife Margot produced two children but suffered several miscarriages along the way. In the end, she decided not to try for any more. Asked if she now used some form of contraception, Margot shared her knowledge of PMT (Prime Ministerial Technique) in typically candid fashion. 'Oh no,' she replied, 'Henry always withdraws in time. Such a noble man!'

The writer Aldous Huxley was regularly unfaithful to his wife, for which she must have been quite relieved if his lovemaking technique was anything like the description offered by one lover, Nancy Cunard. Sleeping with Huxley was, she said, 'like being crawled over by slugs.'

In contrast to Huxley and the prolific Victor Hugo, the French writer Honoré de Balzac was a jealous guardian of his grey matter. Balzac believed that, in each ejaculation, a man lost a certain number of brain cells along with his semen. As he hated the thought of letting his creative potential go to such waste, he would deliberately cut short his liaisons with prostitutes, just before the point of release. Unfortunately, one night his self-control let him down. What must have been a rare moment of satisfaction soon turned to regret, as he emerged from the brothel the next morning complaining that he had 'lost' a novel.

Woody Allen paid homage to this historic orgasm in the film *Annie Hall*. Wrestling in bed with Diane Keaton, Woody releases a happy sigh, then murmurs: 'As Balzac said, "There goes another novel"' . . .'

After the death of her beloved Albert, Queen Victoria spent the remaining thirty-nine years of her life in perpetual mourning. Among other things, she certainly missed him in bed. Bertie was still alive when she gave birth to their ninth child, Beatrice. Rather than aim for double figures, the royal physician suggested that it would be safest for Victoria not to have any more children. 'Oh, Sir James,' she replied, 'am I to have no more fun in bed?' After her own death in 1901, parts of her diary were destroyed, due to their saucy references to the Royals' love-life.

A different picture was painted by Charles Greville – the sort of source for a royal story that the press would now pay blood for. He claimed that the wedding night activities between Victoria and Albert were over far too quickly, and that they'd have to wake up their ideas if they were ever to produce a Prince of Wales. Bearing in mind Victoria's own views and the number of children she and Bertie produced, Charles Greville would seem to have been about as reliable a source as today's sensational storytellers.

Hollywood blonde Jean Harlow had a nightmare honeymoon with her husband Paul Bern, a producer, director and scriptwriter whose credits included a film called *The Marriage Circle*. Bern was a quiet but popular man, yet on their wedding night he beat Harlow with a cane and left teethmarks on her legs that were far more severe than impassioned love-bites. The reason? When it came to wedding tackle, Bern was extremely short; Jean's reaction to this or else his own sense of shame must have led to the beating. Although they maintained a façade of newly-wedded bliss, they fought often and Jean wanted a divorce as soon as respectably possible. Two months after the wedding, Paul attempted to consummate the marriage using a sex-aid, with disastrous results. That night, after writing her a note apologizing for his behaviour, Paul Bern shot himself.

66

**Men survive earthquakes, epidemics, illness and every kind of suffering, but always the most poignant tragedy was, is and will be the tragedy of the bedroom.**

LEO TOLSTOY

Many a quarrel between F. Scott Fitzgerald and his wife Zelda revolved around sex. When Zelda complained that Scott's penis was too small to satisfy her, Fitzgerald consulted Ernest Hemingway, literature's Mr Macho, for a second opinion. A bemused Hemingway took a look and assured Fitzgerald that he had nothing to worry about. The way Hemingway saw it, Zelda was simply trying to destroy her husband. He suggested Fitzgerald should sleep with some other women to restore his confidence. With this in mind, Fitzgerald bought some condoms, but when Zelda found them the result was another furious row. Shortly afterwards, the increasingly loopy Zelda accused Scott of having an affair with Hemingway . . .

66

**The universal preoccupation with sex has become a nuisance.**

F. SCOTT FITZGERALD

Due to Eleanor Roosevelt's strait-laced attitude, US President-to-be Franklin D. Roosevelt very quickly found marriage a sexually frustrating arrangement. Curiously, his suppressed libido found an outlet in sleepwalking. Devout Freudians would certainly raise an eyebrow at the thought of Roosevelt, in his sleep, cranking up an imaginary car at the end of the bed. Even more obvious sexual connotations lay in his words on the night that Eleanor woke to see him standing on a chair, reaching for something. What was he doing, she asked. Trying to get a book, he said. Wouldn't it be better to wait till morning, she suggested. 'Why is it,' said the tetchy sleeptalker, 'when there is something I want to do, you always tell me that I can do it another time?'

The Swedish playwright August Strindberg found relationships with women so difficult that he had to keep practising. He eventually married three times, and each time it ended in tears. Frida, his second wife, woke up in the middle of her wedding night to find her new husband throttling her! Roused from her sleep by a sudden, urgent need to breathe, she somehow fought him off, then demanded an explanation. Strindberg was profoundly sorry; half asleep, he had mistaken her for his first wife – the only wife, he assured her, whom he wished to kill. This didn't entirely set her mind at rest. As Frida later commented, 'I didn't get to sleep again for quite a while.'

It was a happy scene at the railway station, as a host of well-wishers waved off the newly married Peter Ilyich Tchaikovsky and his wife Antonina, but for Tchaikovsky the wedding had been nothing but 'ghastly spiritual torture'. As a highly sensitive homosexual, he was far from eager to consummate the marriage. Two days into the honeymoon, he wrote to his brother, Modest, also a homosexual: 'When the train started I was ready to scream; sobs choked me.' To make matters worse, Antonina was something of a nymphomaniac. Within nine weeks, the marriage was over.

A far more successful union was the one between Sir Arthur Conan Doyle and his second wife Jean. 'After twenty-three years of married life,' Jean reflected, 'whenever I heard my husband's dear voice in the distance, or he came into the room, something radiant seemed to enter and permeate the atmosphere.' It is this happy couple who hold the record for the longest honeymoon. In more expansive terms than Sherlock Holmes could ever manage, Sir Arthur once claimed: 'My honeymoon began on the day I was wed, and will continue right through eternity.'

# CHAPTER TEN

# CAUGHT IN THE ACT

## *When private enterprise goes public*

*T*here are a number of precautions that lovers must take if they wish to avoid being caught in the act:

1. Check all doors and windows are bolted. (Unless in a lift.*)

2. Check the cupboards. If Lord Lambton had done so, he would have found a two-way mirror (see Point 3), the lady's husband and a camera.

3. Check behind *all* mirrors, particularly if they are above the bed, as one in Errol Flynn's house was – a two-way source of much entertainment to spectators in the room above.

4. *Double*-check that your lover's spouse is far, far away.

*If you *must* do it in a lift, follow the example of Derek Jameson and his first wife Jackie, who kept the door open and pounded away on the top floor, whilst a growing crowd below tried to work out why the lift wasn't responding to the button.

5.    *Treble*-check that your own spouse is far, far, far away.
      Unless, by an uncanny coincidence, your lover *is* your
      spouse.

*The trouble with following this sort of procedure is that it kills
impulse. Breaking off from a passionate embrace to conduct a
thorough examination of all the danger-points would have a cooling
effect on the most hot-blooded of lovers. Which is why many throw
caution to the winds – the element of danger can even add extra spice!*

Another way to keep intruders at bay is to have a friend
posted outside. James II employed a courtier who was so good
at his job that, one night, he even managed to turn away the
lady in question's husband. And a loyal Beatles fan did her
best to help when Paul McCartney was entertaining a young
lady named Francie Schwartz. Jane Asher, Paul's mate at the
time, was supposed to be away on tour with the Bristol Old
Vic, so when she unexpectedly turned up at the house, one of
the girls hanging around outside buzzed Paul on the entry-
phone to warn him. 'Pull the other one!' laughed Paul before
returning to Francie. He was not in such a jovial mood a
minute later; and nor was Jane, as she entered to find Ms
Schwartz clad in nothing but Paul's dressing gown. Jane stormed out and, shortly afterwards, her mum was round to pick
up her things.

Whilst acting together in the Nick Roeg film *Performance*,
Mick Jagger and James Fox found they had quite different
ideas about how to spend breaks in filming. While Roeg was
setting up the next shot, Fox decided to pop into his co-star's
dressing room for a quick chat. However, chatting was far
from Jagger's mind, as Fox wandered in on a quite separate

'performance' starring Mick Jagger and actress Anita Pallenberg, who was meant to be guitarist Keith Richard's leading lady.

Waiting for the Jaggers and Pallenbergs of this world to reappear on the film set may be one of the chores of film-making, but at least it does nothing to interfere with the finished product. Behind-the-scenes activity during a stage play has more serious repercussions. Jerome Bonaparte never matched his big brother Napoleon's achievements on the battlefield, but his conquests elsewhere gained him particular notoriety. Napoleon made him King of Westphalia, hoping to inspire in him some sense of responsibility, but this just provided Jerome I with more luxurious surroundings in which to lead his life of lusty leisure. At the theatre, the royal box offered the perfect place to entertain pretty girls during the interval. One night he even invited an actress up from the stage between acts. They were having such a good time that they failed to notice the curtain going up for the resumption of the play. Missing one of the leading players, the drama soon ground to a halt. As the puzzled audience checked their programmes, the unbilled performance came to a satisfying conclusion and Jerome's new friend hurried back down to the stage to pick up her cue.

> ❝ **I get very sexually excited on stage. It's not just an act.**
>
> PRINCE

> ❝ **When I act I don't make love and when I make love I don't act.**
>
> MAE WEST

A much smaller audience witnessed the lusty author Victor Hugo in the throes of passion with a young laundry maid. When his grandson walked in on the scene, Hugo, far from knocked out of his rhythm, welcomed him with the immodest words, 'that's what they call genius'. At a venerable eighty years of age, there was plenty of life in the old dog yet.

Not all dogs are so lucky. There wasn't much life left in Pips, D. H. Lawrence's faithful hound, after his master caught him in a compromising position with a passing bitch. Lawrence, impotent himself, separated the pair and, in a jealous fury, started kicking Pips until a friend of Lawrence's came to the poor dog's rescue.

Robinson

" **Familiarity breeds contempt — and children.**

MARK TWAIN

Whilst his wife kept house and raised their young family in Wales, David Lloyd George was busy pursuing his parliamentary career and the wife of the President of the Welsh Presbyterian Association. At some time or other, Lloyd George's young son Richard must have caught the two of them in a tender moment, because he later asked his mother why Daddy had been 'eating Mrs Davies's hand'. In the dust-up that followed, Lloyd George offered the excuse that he felt neglected by his wife. As a result, the whole family moved up from Wales to Wandsworth Common, and Lloyd George gave up dining on Mrs Davies.

As with Lloyd George, Lord Palmerston's reputation as a ladies' man never held him back from becoming Prime Minister. Palmerston even got away with trying to sneak into a lady's bedroom while staying the night as a guest of Queen Victoria at Windsor Castle! Mrs Brand, whose room the philandering Palmerston tried to enter, immediately informed Her Majesty, who most definitely was not amused.

As their son and heir, Edward VII gave Victoria and Albert even more cause for moral outrage than their Prime Minister. It was not for nothing that Henry James once referred to him as 'Edward the Caresser'. One lady to enjoy Edward's caresses was the French Princess Jeanne de Sagan. The two of them were keeping each other company in the warmest possible way when her young son popped his head round the bedroom door. His mum and the then Prince of Wales were having too much fun to notice the appalled youngster crossing the room, picking up Edward's clothes and throwing them out of the window into the fountains below. Soon afterwards, Edward's satisfied smile had turned into a furious scowl. Once his clothes had been recovered, the Prince of Snappy Dressers was obliged to return home in a borrowed pair of trousers, dry but a couple of sizes too small.

> **Music and women I cannot but give way to, whatever my business is.**
>
> SAMUEL PEPYS

Revenge can be exacted in a single, inspired moment, but sometimes the offender is made to pay day after day and night after night. Samuel Pepys's wife did not let her husband off lightly, after she had caught him with his hand beneath the skirts of their maid, Deb Willet. His diary entry for 25 October 1668 describes the scene:

> ... and after supper, to have my head combed by Deb, which occasioned the greatest sorrow to me that ever I knew in this world; for my wife, coming up suddenly, did find me imbracing the girl con my hand sub su coats; and endeed, I was with my main in her cunny ...'

### GLOSSARY OF PEPYSIAN TERMS

con – with; sub – under; su – her; coats – petticoat; main – hand; cunny – er ...

Many a furious row followed. The maid had to go, and Mrs Pepys took to waking Sam up in the middle of the night to have another yell at him. On one occasion, she even held red hot coals in front of his face while he slept, causing him to dream that he was burning in the fires of hell. And yet, as can often happen, the conflict put unexpected zest into their sex life ...

> 14 November 1668: And so at night home to supper, and there did sleep with great content with my wife. I must here remember that I have lain with my moher (wife) as a husband more times since this falling-out than in I believe twelve months before – and with more pleasure to her than I think in all the time of our marriage before.

Before any twentieth-century ladies start fantasizing about Pepys the great lover ... it's been said that he never took a bath in his whole life.

Pepys's king at the time, Charles II, was one of Britain's most wayward monarchs, but was fortunate in having, as his Queen, one of the world's most understanding wives. Once, when Charles was entertaining a young lady in his bedchamber, Queen Catherine strolled into the room without knocking. In a flurry of bedclothes, Charles did his best to look innocent and alone, but when Catherine spotted an unfamiliar silk slipper on the floor, she just looked at him, laughed and politely left the room.

Next in line, James II learnt from his big brother's mistake and had a courtier stand outside the bedroom door while he made merry with a certain Lady Southesk. However, they were as good as caught in the act when her husband returned home unexpectedly. The courtier on sentry duty, not recognizing Lord Southesk, gave him a knowing wink and told him that he'd better find a different mistress for the night as this one was already taken. Southesk, though fuming, had no choice but to retreat.

When caught in a compromising situation, kings can get away with more than most. In Verdi's opera *Rigoletto*, the character of the womanizing Duke of Mantua was largely based on the real-life François I of France. On one occasion, entering the house of a lawyer for a late-night liaison with the man's wife, François was surprised to find the husband at home after all. The lawyer was even more surprised to find himself playing host to the King of France, particularly at such an unearthly hour! François, as used to this sort of dilemma as any man could be, coolly told the lawyer that he had always wanted to meet him, but court life being so hectic, this was the only time he could manage to call! The lawyer was probably smart enough to realize the true reason for the King's visit but, since he was also smart enough to know what was good for him, he accepted the story without a murmur.

For unlikely excuses, Chico Marx capped even François I when he was caught kissing a chorus girl. 'I wasn't kissing her,' Chico protested, 'I was whispering in her mouth . . .'

Henry II was so fond of one mistress, Rosamund Clifford, that he had a maze of secret passages built into his castle so that he could sneak off to her chamber for late-night liaisons. He was found out though, when a thread from a ball of floss caught on his spur and unravelled behind him. His wife, Queen Eleanor, followed the trail. And at the end of this yarn . . .? According to the various stories told, Rosamund was poisoned or stabbed at Queen Eleanor's command or, less fun for storytellers but more happily for Rosamund, she retired to a convent.

John Churchill, Ist Duke of Marlborough and Commander of the victorious British troops against the French at Blenheim, was in his early twenties when he embarked on a foolhardy three-year affair with Charles II's own mistress, Barbara, Lady Castlemaine. His talent for keeping a cool head in dangerous circumstances, which was to serve him so well in battle, was put to an early test when the King called unexpectedly on Barbara. Swiftly gathering his clothes, young Churchill leapt from her first floor bedroom window to avoid a situation that may well have changed the course of his military career, and, perhaps, British history as well. Barbara, impressed with his quick thinking and relieved at their escape, rewarded him with £500.

When the Duke of Argyll divorced the Duchess in 1963, he threatened to name numerous well-connected gentlemen as co-respondents. One compromising piece of evidence was a photograph that included a naked man whose head had been cut out of the picture. It was, claimed the Duke, a Minister in Her Majesty's Government. Lord Denning, to his credit, was unable to identify the man from the evidence before him, so he asked a top doctor to inspect the Minister's private parts, to see if they matched up with those in the photo. 'It has been demonstrated to my entire satisfaction,' pronounced Denning after the examination, 'that the "unknown" man in the photographs was not this Minister.'

**❝ To err is human, but it feels divine.**

MAE WEST

Ten years later, a different Cabinet Minister was more comprehensively captured on film and dispatched into the political wilderness. Lord Lambton was parliamentary under-secretary in the Ministry of Defence when his relationship with a call-girl named Norma Levy hit the headlines. It had been a straightforward, business-like affair between a prostitute and an anonymous wealthy client until his Lordship was careless enough to pay her by cheque. Norma's husband, Colin, immediately realized that here were the makings of a political scandal which the newspapers would pay thousands for. He also realized he could considerably raise the price by providing exclusive photographs of the liaison. And so, in the bedroom of their Maida Vale flat, he installed a new wardrobe, complete with two-way mirror. Shortly afterwards, while Col snapped away from behind the mirror and fought off any twinges of cramp, his wife, Lord Lambton and a black lady named Kim frolicked on the bed, then unwound with a joint. Lambton talked contentedly of his love of 'the weed' unaware that not only was he on 'Candid Camera', but that the cuddly teddy-bear in the corner of the room had a tape-recorder whirring inside its belly. His political career was as good as over. After his resignation from office, Lambton had some sound advice for his fellow politicians and indeed any other gorger of forbidden fruit – 'Don't get caught.'

# CHAPTER ELEVEN

# THE ETERNAL TRIANGLE

*Two's company,
three's a . . . dultery*

Life on the road offers the married man many temptations –
all the rock stars who have fallen for the lure of a groupie will
be able to sympathize with Chairman Mao Tse-tung. As he
travelled over China, organizing the peasants into revolution,
he admitted that he was susceptible to 'voluptuous feelings' at
the sight of a pretty girl. While his wife, Yang Kai-hui, did her
work for the revolution at home, the touring Mao took up
with the girl who was to become his second wife, Ho Tzu-
chen. They married after the brave Yang Kai-hui had been
tortured and executed by Mao's enemies, for refusing to give
them a list of Mao's followers. Mao ran his wives in relay,
testing each one out as a mistress first. His third marriage to
the actress Chiang Ching was finally made possible by sending
Ho Tzu-chen to Russia for 'medical treatment'. In the
seventies the tables were turned, as rumours spread that Chiang Ching had embarked on a passionate affair with the
world's number one ping-pong player, Chuang Tse-tung.

> **I don't know of any young man, black or white, who doesn't have a girlfriend besides his wife. Some have four sneaking around.**

MOHAMMED ALI

How can a man commit adultery with his wife? H. G. Wells attempted it when his second wife, Catherine, showed far less interest in sex than he had bargained for. After a few years of frustration he returned to his first wife, whom he had divorced in order to marry Catherine, and begged her to sleep with him. She refused.

Sir Robert Walpole, Britain's first Prime Minister, had many affairs during his unhappy thirty-seven-year marriage to Catherine Shorter. Any politician caught with a call-girl or pregnant secretary will find comfort in the complete absence of damage caused to 'Wally's' career by his various misdemeanours. Such was his reputation that there were even rumours that he and Queen Caroline, wife of George II, were lovers. However, twenty-stone men were probably not her type. On one occasion, when Caroline asked why Walpole seemed distressed, she was assured by an adviser that it was not over a matter of state importance, but because his mistress was ill. The Queen expressed herself happy that he kept himself busy in his spare time, though surprised if Walpole truly believed that any girl could love such an overweight and repulsive creature as himself for any reason other than money.

> **Thou shalt not commit adultery ...
> unless in the mood.**

W. C. FIELDS

Queen Victoria once said that one of Albert's finest qualities was the way he never paid attention to other women. At which Lord Melbourne, her Prime Minister, nodded his head and casually remarked that that sort of thing tended to come later. Once again, Victoria's amusement level hit zero. 'I shan't forgive you for that,' she told him.

## MARX AND ENGELS IN SECRET LOVE-CHILD TRIANGLE!!

In different times, the co-authors of *The Communist Manifesto* might well have found their homes besieged by eager press reporters. The unplanned pregnancy occurred while Karl Marx and his wife Jenny were living on the breadline in Soho, with their young family and their devoted maidservant Lenchen. Jenny was away in Holland, begging for money from Karl's uncle, when an evening chess game between Karl and Lenchen ended in some serious mating. After Jenny had been home for a few months, Lenchen's pregnancy became increasingly obvious, so Marx talked his best pal, Friedrich Engels, into taking the blame. For all Friedrich's role-playing, it is quite possible that Jenny suspected the truth. Still, Engels kept the secret and Jenny kept a stiff upper lip. Poor Lenchen, however, did not keep the baby, giving it away to a foster mother instead.

> **I do not trust men who run after every woman — this is not the way to win revolutions. Revolution needs concentration, a heightening of forces. The wild excesses of sexual life are reactionary symptoms.**
>
> LENIN

A friend in need . . . When T. S. Eliot and his young wife Vivien were looking for somewhere to stay, the philandering philosopher Bertrand Russell offered them space in his London flat. When Eliot was away, the friendship between 'Dirty Bertie' and Vivien blossomed; even after the Eliots had a place of their own, the two would go out for lunch together. All good intentions, Russell had decided that the relationship would be strictly platonic but, not for the first time, his great mind gave in to the temptations of the flesh.

> **I never was attached to that great sect,**
> **Whose doctrine is that each one should**
> **   select**
> **Out of the crowd a mistress or a friend,**
> **And all the rest, though fair and wise,**
> **   commend**
> **To cold oblivion.**
>
> PERCY BYSSHE SHELLEY 'Epipsychidion'

B onnie and Clyde are names that will always stand together in the history of crime; in the history of sex, though, it would be more accurate to think of Bonnie and Clyde and William . . . Bonnie Parker's first marriage had not been a success, the State enforcing separation by sentencing her husband to ninety-nine years for murder. Her new partner, Clyde Barrow, also found himself in prison soon after they met, but Bonnie helped him out, so to speak, by smuggling a gun to him. The gang's first recruit was William Jones, who left his job at a petrol station to pump lead into people instead of cars. Since Clyde was a sensitive, somewhat effeminate sort of bloke, he found it hard to keep up with Bonnie's insatiable sexual appetite. It therefore fell to William, as a faithful gang member, to keep Bonnie happy.

James I was very much a man's man, although he did survive a six-month bout of heterosexuality after his marriage to Anne of Denmark. Philip Herbert, one of James's 'favourites' at court, had rather less than six months alone with his bride, as the gay monarch bounced into bed to join Philip and his new wife on the morning after their wedding night.

James's grandson, Charles II, was considerably more enthusiastic in his pursuit of women. One of his mistresses, Barbara, Lady Castlemaine, was expecting their second child when he married Catherine of Braganza in 1662. Catherine had no choice but to put up with the steady stream of females who warmed the King's bed. Lady Castlemaine also had to accept that she was not the only mistress in Charles's life. At one time, Charles was very keen on his cousin Frances Stuart, whom Lady Castlemaine soon befriended. Indeed they became such good friends that Charles once discovered the two ladies in bed together. He happily leapt in to join them, but to his annoyance Frances leapt out before he could relieve her of her virginity.

> **The chief occupation of my life has been to cultivate the pleasures of the senses. Nothing has ever meant as much to me as that. Feeling myself born for the fair sex, I have always loved it, and have been loved in return as often as possible.**
>
> CASANOVA

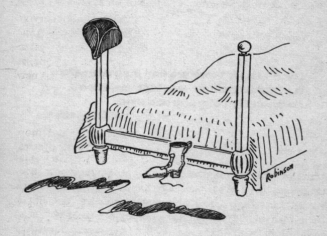

Believe it or not, Casanova wanted to be a priest in his early years. But a pretty girl distracted him during his first sermon and he never finished it. Disconsolately leaving the church, the chaste failure was comforted by a pair of young sisters, named Nanette and Marton. With the charm that was to serve him so well, he somehow convinced them that he would not lay a finger on them if they would just keep him company in his lonely bed. By the next morning, the three virgins were virgins no more.

In Bob Dylan's film *Renaldo and Clara*, the leading man lives with his wife, then lives with a girlfriend, and then lives with both of them. In real life, Bob Dylan lived with his wife Sara, then lived with Joan Baez, and then lived with both of them.

Marilyn Monroe and Yves Montand enjoyed a fling whilst making a film away from their respective spouses, Arthur Miller and Simone Signoret. The title of the film? *Let's Make Love.*

**I don't think there are any men who are faithful to their wives. Men are such a combination of good and evil.**

JACKIE ONASSIS

One of the twentieth century's most illustrious love-triangles involved Maria Callas, Jackie Kennedy and Aristotle Onassis. Onassis, a Greek shipping tycoon and one of the richest men in the world, had enjoyed a passionate extra-marital affair with opera star Callas, but when both their divorces came through in the early sixties, Maria was far keener than Ari on the idea of their marrying. When Ari married Jackie Kennedy instead, Maria was heartbroken. Richard Burton saw Callas in 1968 and noted that she wore dark glasses most of the time – 'perhaps she cries a lot'. Burton was sympathetic to Maria's plight though he had to admit that 'without knowing her, and if I had the choice, I'm afraid I'd elect for Jackie Kennedy'. However, it would seem that Ari (and Burton) made the wrong choice. Soon Ari was seeing Maria again. Jackie fell out with the Onassis family, and when Ari died her share of the will was worth only a few million dollars. Still, it was more than Maria ever got. She died alone in Paris, in 1977.

Robinson

**Had we never lov'd sae kindly,
Had we never lov'd sae blindly,
Never met — or never parted,
We had ne'er been broken-hearted.**
ROBBIE BURNS

Robbie Burns was unstinting in his research on the subject of love and heartbreak. As his exceptionally tolerant wife, Jean, once remarked: 'Oor Rab should have had twa wives.' 'Twa' was probably an underestimate. Still, Robbie was extremely fortunate in the wife he *did* have; she even brought up one of his illegitimate children as part of the family.

Mark Antony's wife Octavia showed similar generosity of spirit after the deaths of her husband and his lover, Cleopatra. In an unusual variation on the single-parent family, Octavia, 'whose virtue and whose general graces speak that which none else can utter' (Shakespeare, *Antony and Cleopatra*) took on the responsibility of bringing up Antony and Cleopatra's children.

George Lewes was still a married man when he started living with the writer George Eliot. However, the Lewes's marriage was based on a liberal agreement that allowed extramarital relationships for both parties. Mrs Lewes took more advantage of this arrangement than Mr Lewes did; she produced several children who were not his, but he nobly provided for them all the same. When the two Georges eloped in 1854, one writer, Thomas Woolner, described the happy couple as 'stinkpots of humanity'.

66
**The woman who deceives her husband is the destruction of her house.**

WILLIAM THE CONQUEROR

Another couple of stinkpots, Peter Finch and Vivien Leigh enjoyed a torrid two-year affair while Ms Leigh was married to Laurence Olivier. Finally, after a strained dinner at the Oliviers' home, Peter and Larry adjourned to the library to talk it out man to man. They had yet to reach a conclusion when Vivien – as wilful as Scarlett O'Hara, the part she played in *Gone With the Wind* – burst into the room and announced she was going to bed; which one of them was going to sleep with her? Shortly afterwards, Peter Finch left the Oliviers' home, never to return.

## DECISIONS, DECISIONS...

Pablo Picasso was painting *Guernica*, his impassioned masterpiece depicting the horrors of the Spanish Civil War, and his girlfriend Dora Maar was taking photos of the work in progress, when Picasso's wife, Marie-Thérèse, turned up unexpectedly and told Dora to go. She refused. Marie-Thérèse turned to Picasso. 'It's your decision,' she told him. 'Which of us should go?' Picasso, whose chief concern was to get on with his work, simply could not make up his mind – he liked them both in their separate ways. With an unhelpful shrug, he told them to fight it out amongst themselves. So, while Dora and Marie-Thérèse went for each other's throats, Picasso calmly resumed painting his protest against violence, pain and suffering.

> **I've had lots of offers but I've never been tempted. Affairs are an immense waste of time.**
>
> CILLA BLACK

Mary Queen of Scots was already enjoying the company of an Italian singer named David Rizzio when she married Lord Darnley in 1565. From the humble depths of bass singer in a court quartet, Rizzio rose to the position of secretary, with special responsibility for her correspondence with France. Soon rumours were spreading that Rizzio – for all his expertise with French letters – was father of the child Mary was carrying. Less than a year after the wedding, Darnley and a fellow conspirator dragged Rizzio away from the dinner table he was sharing with Mary and stabbed him to death. Mary, six months pregnant, reacted with remarkable calm. 'No more tears,' she said, 'I will think upon a revenge.' Within a year, Darnley was dead, the victim of a plot between Mary and her latest lover, the Earl of Bothwell.

> **A cock is a divining rod that finds trouble for men.**
>
> ROGER MOORE

A more sophisticated and appropriate revenge was exacted by a cuckolded shopkeeper against the French philanderer,

King François I. The shopkeeper's wife had been invited to the Louvre, supposedly to meet the Queen, but this was only a ruse to get her into the King's carriage which then transported her to one of his secret love nests in the Bois de Boulogne. On returning home, she told her husband that the Queen wished to keep her at court. Immediately suspicious, the husband pretended to believe her and gave his assent, but after asking around, he soon discovered the true reason for his wife's absences. His response was eccentric, but effective. Previously a clean-living, upright citizen, he embarked on an active tour of Paris's least hygienic whorehouses and it was not long before he was experiencing an uncomfortable itch in his breeches. Shortly afterwards, via their mutual bed-partner, a vigorous strain of venereal disease had made its home in the royal groin.

# CHAPTER TWELVE

# CAUSING A SCENE

*Tiffs, rows and (sometimes) reconciliations*

$L$iz Taylor and Richard Burton liked to hurl insults at each other, Edith Piaf preferred inanimate objects; George IV humiliated his wife in public, Nelson merely humiliated his in front of embarrassed dinner guests. Couples who never argue are rare indeed. Before his marriage to Marta, Sigmund Freud estimated they could reasonably expect to have some kind of quarrel at least once a week. As things turned out, the only argument between them that Freud noted in his journals was about mushrooms and whether they should be cooked with or without their stalks. For the likes of Stalin, Mozart and Humphrey Bogart, domestic life was not so smooth!

There is no better way to deal with an insult than to turn it on its head and toss it back at the insulter. One old flame of William Pitt the Younger's was the domineering Duchess of Gordon, who, upon meeting him for the first time in quite a while, asked whether he still talked as much nonsense as he had when they'd lived together. 'I do not know, madam, whether I talk so much nonsense,' he replied. 'I certainly don't hear so much.'

Winston Churchill and Lady Astor had such a bitchy relationship that they really should have married. But the idea held no appeal for either of them. Lady Astor once informed Churchill that if he were her husband, she would poison his coffee. 'If you were my wife,' replied Churchill, 'I'd drink it.'

'Nobody turns insults to her advantage more swiftly or more cleverly than Lady Elizabeth.' When Richard Burton called Elizabeth Taylor's hands 'large and ugly and red and masculine', she calmly hit back by suggesting he buy her a 69-carat ring, to make her hands look smaller and less ugly. In his diary, Burton wrote, 'that insult last night is going to cost me.' It did – over a million dollars!

> **Our natures do not inspire domestic tranquillity.**
>
> RICHARD BURTON

For Taylor and Burton, sarcasm, abuse and stony silence were all elements of their favourite competitive sport. In one of his notebooks, Richard Burton described a typical row, about a lingering smell in the bathroom. When he suggested that Liz might be responsible, she curtly told him to fuck off. Rich continued reading in the bedroom until, twenty minutes later, Liz appeared at the doorway and said, 'I dislike you and hate you.' 'Goodnight,' replied Rich, changing into his dressing gown and strolling off to read in a spare room, 'have a good sleep.' 'You too,' said Liz. The important thing about this dialogue, according to Burton, was not the choice of words but the way they were spoken: 'instinct with venomous malice'.

Frédéric Chopin, composer of so many romantic melodies, was also a master of the long moody silence. George Sand once wrote of his sulking: 'The day before yesterday he spent the whole day without speaking a word to a soul. Was he ill? Has somebody annoyed him? Have I said something to upset him? I shall never know . . .' However, she was aware of the part such silences can play in a battle of wills. 'I must not let him think he is the master here,' she wrote. 'He would be all the more touchy in future.'

The angry young playwright John Osborne came up against similar silences in one of his marriages. When he could take no more, he exploded, as only Osborne could, with the words: 'I'm sick of all your mute attrition!'

> **66**
> **Cruelty, possessiveness and petty jealousy are traits you develop when in love.**
>
> NOËL COWARD

It must have given Lord Nelson a perverse sort of pleasure to have his wife invite his mistress, Lady Hamilton, and her husband to a dinner at their house in Dover Street. Even more perverse was his behaviour towards Lady Nelson during the meal. At one stage, Lady Hamilton excused herself from the table, saying she did not feel well. When Lady Nelson did not get up to attend to her, Nelson gave her a long, loud and humiliating ticking-off. Rather than stay with her husband and their embarrassed guests, Lady Nelson left the room and found Lady Hamilton throwing up into a handbasin. The hostess dutifully held the basin as it filled with reminders of dinner. What she probably didn't know at the time was that Lady Hamilton was pregnant – with Lord Nelson's child.

In 1972, Mick and Bianca Jagger shared a rather silly row with some invited guests at a leaving party for Shirley Arnold, who had been running the Rolling Stones fan club since 1963. Mick had got there first and presented Shirley with an expensively bejewelled cross, which he said was 'from both of us'. Then Bianca turned up with a large bottle of perfume which she handed to Shirley with the same words, 'from both of us'. Instead of laughing about the mix-up, Mick and Bianca chose to quarrel, providing the party with an unexpected cabaret.

Mao Tse-tung's second wife Ho Tzu-chen was said to have 'the temper of a Hunanese donkey'. Certainly she thought nothing of threatening the future leader of the People's Republic of China with a stick of broken furniture, and he, showing due respect for the equality of the sexes, would wield a chair-leg in return. Disputes with his third wife were of a colder, more rational nature. Even after their divorce, the politically ambitious Chiang Ching wanted to use their relationship to further her own career; however, Mao refused to grant her an audience. Instead, he sent her some advice – she should be reading more, in particular the great works of Marx, Lenin, and . . . Mao.

'Uncle Joe' Stalin was not the kind of man to pick a quarrel with. Even his second wife came to a violent end after arguing with him at a party. Opinions differ as to how the row started. Was it just because he'd addressed her in a surly manner? Or did they quarrel about one of his lovers? Or, most likely to start a *blazing* row, did he throw a lighted cigarette at her, which dropped down the cleavage of her dress? Whatever the case, both were soon storming out of the party. The events of the next few hours are something of a mystery; the only undisputed fact is that by morning she was dead. A gun was found just beside the body. If it was murder, the statisticians can add yet one more killing to Stalin's credit, but most probably it was his wife's own finger that pulled the trigger, either deliberately or by accident.

Q: What do Derek Jameson and Humphrey Bogart have in common – besides the obvious rugged good looks and charm?

A: *Both were once stabbed by unhinged lovers.*

Derek Jameson tried to break the news gently as he ended his affair with a German girlfriend, but when she drew a pair of scissors out of her handbag, he was terrified that she was going to stab herself. He needn't have worried, since the scissors soon found their true target, just below his rib-cage. There was a lot of blood, but fortunately this wound, the most severe he suffered whilst on National Service, turned out to be just a scratch.

Humphrey Bogart's third wife, Mayo, enjoyed some success as an actress in her own right before settling down to a life of booze and brawls as the female half of the Battling Bogarts (as they were known to friends and long-suffering neighbours). Invariably Mayo was jealous of Humphrey's leading ladies; while he was filming *To Have and Have Not* with Lauren Bacall, Mayo strode into the studio and loudly enquired how he was getting on with 'that poor child half your age'. Some squabbles fizzled out with barely a plate broken; other rows led to Mayo setting the house on fire, slashing her own wrists, and stabbing Bogey in the back with a carving knife. As with Jameson, the wound was only a passing inconvenience. 'Only went in a little way,' said Bogart to the doctor doing the stitches.

Another battling Hollywood couple were Lupe Velez, 'The Mexican Spitfire', and Johnny 'Tarzan' Weissmuller. If that sounds like a billing for a professional wrestling contest, it's entirely appropriate. Their public rows were ignited on more than one occasion by Lupe's favourite party piece, the simple act of throwing her dress over her head. Johnny never found this funny, and what added to the rage of a man famous for wearing nothing but jungle underwear was the fact that, when Lupe performed this trick, it was immediately apparent that she'd left her underwear at home.

Heaven knows how Mozart would have coped with being married to Lupe. He worked himself up into enough of a stew when his wife-to-be, Constanze, allowed a young man at a party to measure the calves of her legs. According to Mozart's irate letter to her, such games were foolish to play at the best of times. If she really had no choice, she should at least have measured her own calves, rather than let a man do it for her.

Roger Moore was gazing at a shapely pair of calves and more besides, before his reverie was shattered by a resounding slap from his wife Luisa. It was the Swinging Sixties, with the mini-skirt all the rage, and into the restaurant where the Moores were dining had walked a girl wearing a particularly mini mini. Moore couldn't help following her with his eyes, until Luisa's brusque intervention. 'What was that for?' asked Moore, rubbing his reddened cheek; after all, he had only been *looking*. 'That's just in case,' Luisa replied.

> " It hasn't been perfect — what marriage
> is? But you can't have everything.
> You've got to keep that in mind,
> otherwise you'll be forever searching.
>
> THERESA RUSSELL

Sophia Loren's Latin temperament has resulted in numerous fits of jealousy over her producer husband Carlo Ponti, even though he is considerably older than she is. Once, while flying over Rome, the plane Ponti was travelling in suddenly dropped several hundred feet and he was thrown from his seat; his ear was cut so badly that he had to have it stitched back into place. When his loving wife came to visit him in hospital, she brought him a magazine to read. Inside the mag was an article linking Ponti's name with another woman. 'Is it true?' she demanded. Ponti told her not to be silly, of course it wasn't. 'I believe you,' she said at last, 'but if I find it *is* true, I'll cut off your other ear.'

If he had been married to a woman like Sophia Loren, David Lloyd George would have been Britain's first earless Prime Minister. For many years, he lived two separate domestic lives, one with his wife and family, the other with his secretary and mistress, Frances Stevenson. But if leading two lives meant enjoying twice the normal pleasures, it also meant twice the rows. Arguments between Lloyd George and Frances usually revolved round the subject of him getting divorced and marrying her. In one attempt to goad him into action, Frances threatened to leave him and find herself a millionaire to marry. Lloyd George surprised her by agreeing enthusiastically – if Frances were to marry, it would provide a far better cover for them to continue their relationship without raising people's suspicions!

> 66 We have lived together in perfect harmony for fifty years. One of us is contentious, combative, and stormy. That is my wife. Then there is the other partner, placid, calm, peaceful and patient. That is me.
>
> DAVID LLOYD GEORGE
> (speaking at their Golden Wedding party)

The epic notes of *Also Sprach Zarathustra* which open the film *2001* in such a grandiose manner were written by one of music's most henpecked husbands. Richard Strauss once claimed that his wife Pauline's combative personality gave him a refreshing break from the praise that was usually showered on him, but it certainly caused him plenty of public embarrassment as well. After a performance of his opera *Feuersnot*, he took several rapturous curtain calls before going up to the box from where Pauline had been watching. 'What did you think of it?' he asked her, beaming with happiness. Pauline exploded; it was a feeble effort, barely worthy of being called an opera, a second-rate rip-off of Wagner . . . 'You thief!' she yelled, 'you disgust me!' When they turned up later in the evening for a banquet to celebrate the opera's opening, the great composer trailed in meekly behind his wife.

On the day of his coronation, George IV arranged for the public humiliation of his estranged wife, Caroline, by giving explicit orders that she be kept out of Westminster Abbey while the ceremony was taking place. George had already tried to force a bill through Parliament declaring the marriage null and void but, after an undignified 'trial', the bill had been dropped. And so George had to wait for his crowning moment, when Caroline arrived at the Abbey and, for all her protestations, was firmly turned away.

Quentin Crisp, loudly proud to be gay, suffered a different public indignity while waiting innocently for a bus. Suddenly, to his horror, a pretty girl flung her arms around him and kissed him. The Naked Civil Servant's lips did not respond to the kiss, but opened only when he had managed to cast her off. 'You had better catch your bus,' he said, readjusting his hair. The girl was an art student at the college where Crisp was modelling and, somehow, had seen him as a potential husband. They exchanged several letters, in which she pleaded for his love and he begged to be left in peace. The poor girl even threatened suicide before she finally got the message – Mr Crisp was not Mr Right.

George Bernard Shaw and his former lover Jenny Patterson engaged in a public row by sending letters to the *Star* newspaper about a murder case in which a man was to be hanged for murdering his ex-mistress. Shaw claimed that such tragic cases would recur 'until we make up our minds as to what a woman's claims exactly are upon a man who, having formerly loved her, now wishes to get free from her society'. Jenny, on the other hand, sympathized with the spurned mistress: 'I know too well the feeling when a girl knows she is no more loved by the one she has given her all to, but is only a thing to be cast aside like a toy which has been tired of.' Shaw fought back on a more analytical level, asserting that the root of the trouble was 'the old theory, that an act of sexual intercourse gives the parties a lifelong claim on one another for better or worse'. As the argument raged in print, readers in the know could see that, fatalities apart, the murder case mirrored Shaw and Patterson's own affair.

> **A sweetheart is a bottle of wine; a wife is a wine bottle.**
>
> BAUDELAIRE

If Edith Piaf ever sang the Rodgers and Hart song 'I Wish I Were in Love Again', she'd have known all about 'the conversation with the flying plates'. Hurling crockery was one of her specialities when battling with her lover Paul Meurisse, a singer himself, though – in Piaf's estimation – not a very good one. He usually reacted to her tantrums with studied indifference, reclining on the bed in his silk dressing-gown and reading a newspaper. Naturally this only made Edith madder. When Paul paid more attention to the radio than to Piaf, it ended up in pieces on the floor. After another flare-up, the distraught Piaf called her friend Tino Rossi and went out for dinner with him. As they ate, she could talk about nothing but her love for Paul. There and then, the noble Rossi set up a reconciliation, phoning Paul from the restaurant and telling him to join them. The moment Paul stepped through the door, Edith grabbed a champagne bottle and charged right for him. Rossi looked on in disbelief as the couple exchanged slaps and tumbled, still fighting, out of the restaurant and into a taxi. The relationship continued in this rollercoaster fashion until Paul was called up for active service and given the softer option of fighting the Nazis.

While Napoleon was away on an eighteen-month stint in Egypt, Josephine looked elsewhere for a bit of fun and found it in a dashing young chap called Hippolyte Charles. When Napoleon heard of this, he was far from pleased, although he soon found consolation with the wife of one of his officers. On Napoleon's return to France, Josephine was so keen to make amends that, instead of waiting at home, she went to meet him. Unfortunately, they missed each other and Napoleon arrived home to find Josephine out and a host of relatives waiting to tell him what a bad girl she had been. By the time she got home, Napoleon had locked himself into his room, where he remained deaf to her pleas and hammerings on the door. Only on the appearance of her children, whom Napoleon loved as if they were his own, did he finally open the door. Josephine promised she would never be unfaithful again, a promise she kept. If Napoleon made a similar promise he didn't keep it, maintaining a steady flow of mistresses until their divorce.

The marriage of Frank Sinatra and movie star Ava Gardner thrived on impassioned bust-ups ... and even more passionate reconciliations. On one occasion, when they were staying at the home of his manager and wife, the hosts sat bemused in the living room whilst shouts and screams rang out from the bedroom above. Then a door slammed and Frank stormed down the stairs. However, Ava was not alone for long. Once she had decided it was time to make up, she did it *her* way, spraying enough of Frank's favourite perfume around the landing for it to waft down the stairs and seduce him nostril first, back up to the bedroom. The happy couple were not seen again for several hours.

> **The problems were never in the bedroom. We were always great in bed. The trouble usually started on the way to the bidet.**
>
> AVA GARDNER

A tiff between Cilla Black and her manager Bobby Willis ended in the perfect reconciliation. They had been together for a few years without bothering to marry, until one evening, while eating at a restaurant, they become embroiled in a petty argument. As the argument swelled to a row, a friend remarked that they sounded like a typical married couple. It was then that they decided to wed.

# CHAPTER THIRTEEN

# SUCH SWEET SORROW

*Separations and divorces –
amicable, acrimonious, out of
court, alimonious*

*Breaking up is hard to do, whether your name is Charles Dickens,
Chris Evert or Louis Armstrong. It's even harder if your name's
Tony Blackburn . . .*

In happier days Charles Dickens had called his wife his
'dearest mouse', but after twenty-three years of marriage he
had come to think of her as 'the skeleton in my domestic
closet'. The relationship came under additional strain when
Hans Christian Andersen came to stay. The original invitation
was for a fortnight, but Andersen felt so at home that he
stayed for five weeks. For all their differences, his hosts gam-
ely smiled their way through this extension but when their
guest finally left, Dickens put a small sign in the spare room:
'Hans Andersen slept in this room for five weeks – which
seemed to the family *ages*!' As for Andersen, he had no idea of
the household tensions he had left behind. 'The family seems

so harmonious,' he wrote to a friend, soon after his return. Within weeks Mr and Mrs Dickens had agreed to separate.

" **When you settle down with the first woman you have, it is rather like going into a sweet shop and only being allowed to have one sweet!**

MALCOLM McLAREN

John Wayne's first marriage, to Josephine, broke up due to Wayne's involvement with another woman. When she found out, Josephine, a devout Catholic, asked the local priest to come round and talk to Wayne. As a result of their conversation, Wayne promised to end the affair, just so long as his wife promised never to ask him about it. Josephine agreed, but the priest was barely out of the front door before she brought the conversation back round to the 'other woman'. It was then that Wayne knew, beyond doubt, that the marriage was over.

Chris Evert and and Jimmy Connors were 'going through some heavy stuff' back in 1975, when Chris played Billie Jean King in the semi-finals of the women's singles at Wimbledon. She was leading 3–0 in the final set, when she happened to look into the crowd and saw Connors sitting next to the sexy actress Susan George. According to Evert, this moment turned the match. 'I freaked out,' she said. 'I couldn't hit a ball after that.' By the time Billie Jean was lifting the championship trophy, after her final victory over Evonne Cawley, the Connors–Evert match was as good as over.

" **After all, my erstwhile dear, My no longer cherished, Need we say it was not love, Just because it perished?**

EDNA ST. VINCENT MILLAY

'Another man' or 'other men' was the pretext for the execution of Anne Boleyn, Henry VIII's second wife. But her main failing in Henry's eyes was her inability to produce a male heir. Another aspect of Anne's character that may have niggled Henry was her appalling behaviour at mealtimes. To have worse table manners than her King must have been quite an achievement, if Charles Laughton's finger lickin', chicken picking performance in *The Private Life of Henry VIII* is anything to go by. Apparently, she so enjoyed eating that she didn't like to stop just because her stomach was full. She would therefore deliberately throw up in order to create room for more food. Consideration was shown to fellow diners by performing this function behind a sheet (held up by a lady in waiting), but the sounds emitted can have left nothing to the imagination.

It's those little things that can ruin a marriage. Ronald Reagan's first wife, the actress Jane Wyman, explained their divorce to friends by saying she couldn't bear to watch 'that damned *King's Row*' any more. *King's Row* was Ronald Reagan's favourite film, starring Ronald Reagan as an amputee ('Where's the rest of me?'), and there were few dinner guests who could escape from the Reagan home without being subjected to a screening. Jane's chief complaint in their divorce case was that Ronnie was too absorbed in politics. Put more simply, she found the man a real bore. 'Ask him the time,' she once told the Hollywood gossip-columnist Sheilah Graham, 'and he'll tell you how the watch is made.'

## SUCH SWEET SORROW

> **If a relationship is just an effort, there's no point in continuing it.**
>
> GLENDA JACKSON

The mighty film director Orson Welles wasn't boring *enough* for Rita Hayworth. 'I adore enormous men,' she said, when asked why she was leaving her brilliant hunk of a husband, 'but I just can't take his genius any more.'

The separation between film director John Huston and Evelyn Keyes was extremely amicable by Hollywood standards. The beautiful Ms Keyes had shared Huston and his San Fernando Valley home with a not so beautiful monkey. They had already decided to separate when Evelyn said, 'John, darling, I'm sorry. One of us has to go . . . it's the monkey or me.' Huston smiled and, after a thoughtful silence, replied, 'Honey, it's you.'

> **You cannot bind a man and a woman together to make them husband and wife. When someone stops caring for your place and wants to leave it, just let them go.**
>
> MAO TSE-TUNG

On 4 July 1973 the Watergate scandal had to share front-page space in US newspapers with a press statement from Elizabeth Taylor . .

> I am convinced it would be a good and constructive idea if Richard and I separated for a while. Maybe we loved each other too much. I never believed such a thing was possible. But we have been in each other's pockets constantly, never being apart but for matters of life and death, and I believe it has caused a temporary breakdown of communication. I believe with all my heart that the separation will ultimately bring us back to where we should be – and that's together . . .

Despite a couple of brief reconciliations, they had to bow to the inevitable. 'I don't approve of divorce as a blank thing,' said Burton, 'but it two people are absolutely sick of each other or the sight of one another bores them, then they should get divorced or separated as soon as possible. That is certain.'

Harrison Ford blames the movie business and a lack of money for the breakup of his first marriage. As a struggling actor, he could never afford to take his wife and sons with him on location. These enforced separations often lasted months and, according to Ford, 'our love tore apart little by little'. He has since married Melissa Mathison, writer of the screenplay of *ET* and mother of Ford's third son, Malcolm. Now that money's not so tight, Harrison can keep his second family together while he's filming.

# SUCH SWEET SORROW

Nick Faldo's line of work was largely responsible for his divorce from his first wife, Melanie. After three years together, Melanie felt there had to be more to marriage than having a husband who spent every daylight hour on the golf course, turned up for dinner and then tumbled into bed. Which just goes to show ... whether your husband is a hopeless but determined amateur or a successful, dedicated professional – being a golf widow is no fun.

Bee Gee Barry Gibb could have found himself divorced if he *hadn't* gone out to work. The millionaire megastar was so apprehensive about recording with mega-megastar Barbra Streisand on her *Guilty* album, that he seriously considered withdrawing from the deal. As it turned out, the partnership could not have been more successful, but it was Barry's wife who ensured it came about; she threatened to divorce him if he turned down the opportunity!

Whatever the feelings between a warring couple, it requires unusual circumstances for one partner to divorce the other purely out of spite. Louis Armstrong and his second wife Lil Hardin (who played piano with Louis in the legendary Hot Five and Hot Seven) separated in 1931, but did not divorce until seven years later, in 1938, when Louis married his third wife, Alpha. According to Lil, Louis hadn't really wanted to marry Alpha and had begged his second wife *not* to give him a divorce, so as to make a third marriage impossible. Years later, reflecting on her decision, Lil said, 'I gave him the divorce just to spite him, I guess.'

Louis Armstrong married four times in all, but was wise enough to keep divorce settlements out of the lawyers' hands. 'Louis didn't believe in alimony,' said his fourth wife, Lucille. 'Whatever he had he gave it all to his ex-wives for a settlement, then he started all over again.'

> 66 **You never realize how short a month is until you pay alimony.**
>
> JOHN BARRYMORE

The actor George Sanders was not so keen to fork out when he and Zsa Zsa Gabor separated. He knew that the only way he could avoid being stung for alimony was by proving his wife's adultery. So, when he learned that Zsa Zsa was 'entertaining' Porfirio Rubirosa, a renowned playboy whose name had been linked with, among others, Eva Perón, he set out for proof. 'This is no time to behave like a gentleman,' he said. 'I am a cad and shall react like one.' One evening in late December, he arrived at the home he had recently shared with Zsa Zsa, accompanied by his lawyer and a photographer. They brought with them a camera, a ladder and a brick. In keeping with the season, the brick was wrapped in cheery Christmas paper but, since Zsa Zsa and Porfirio had left the French windows unlocked, its services were not required. Having climbed up on to the balcony, the assault party burst into the bedroom in an explosion of flashbulbs. The petrified couple covered themselves with sheets, then dashed into the bathroom.

A few minutes later, Zsa Zsa came downstairs to bid George a sheepish good-night. She also gave him a present from under the Christmas tree. George returned the compliment, handing her the giftwrapped brick.

> **❝ I'm a wonderful housekeeper. Every time I get a divorce, I keep the house.**
>
> ZSA ZSA GABOR

When you've been divorced as many times as Zsa Zsa Gabor, you begin to appreciate the importance of timing. In December 1982, she was already telling friends of her plans to divorce, but they were sworn to secrecy, as she wasn't going to leave her husband until after Christmas – she didn't want to be alone for the holidays.

George Sanders' behaviour was that of a perfect gentleman, compared to the way his namesake George I treated his ex-wife, Sophia Dorothea. After she had been discovered having an affair with a Swedish colonel, her lover mysteriously disappeared (missing, presumed hacked into little pieces) and Sophia Dorothea was locked away for the rest of her life. There can have been few harsher divorce settlements. She died at the age of sixty, having spent more than thirty-two years imprisoned in the Castle of Ahlden, without once being allowed to see her own children. Her death came as a blow to George, but only because a fortune-teller had once told him that he would die within a year of his wife. Eight months later, the prophesy came true.

> **❝ No woman came amiss to him if they were very willing and very fat.**
>
> LORD CHESTERFIELD (on George I)

Charlie Chaplin devoted his life to making millions round the world laugh and cry, and to marrying girls several years younger than himself. The older he got, the greater the age-gap became. He found the wife of his dreams at the fourth attempt, when he was 54 and she 18. Of the three divorces that preceded this happy union, it was the split with his second wife, Lita, a mere nineteen years his junior, that turned his hair grey. The divorce complaint which she filed through her lawyers ran to fifty-two pages (an average complaint ran to three or four). Even worse, it recalled their most acrimonious rows and offered intriguing insights into the sex-life of a lovable tramp. *The Complaint of Lita*, a private copy of the original document, was soon available in paperback and became something of a black market bestseller. As the proceedings became more and more bitter, Lita's final weapon was a threat to reveal the names of 'five prominent women' with whom Chaplin had 'liaised' during their marriage. Top of the list was actress Marion Davies, mistress of William Randolph Hearst – the rich, powerful sort of man whom few would choose to offend. At this point, Chaplin gallantly preserved the honour of the ladies involved by coughing up what was then the largest settlement in American legal history. It may be only natural for a wealthy comedian to send his ex-wife laughing all the way to the bank but, as ever, it was the lawyers who had the last laugh, their fees taking a sizeable chunk out of Lita's winnings.

In the 1968 divorce case between Cary Grant and his fourth wife, Dyan Cannon, Dyan complained of the beatings he had given her whilst under the influence of LSD. Two psychiatrists gave evidence in Cary's defence. The first asserted that LSD had actually deepened Grant's sense of compassion for people as well as deepening his understanding of himself. The second psychiatrist said that, on interviewing Grant, he could find no evidence of irrationality or erratic behaviour. Upon the foundation of these testimonies Grant developed the argument that he had beaten Dyan for 'reasonable and adequate causes'. This bizarre line of defence may be judged at least a partial success, since Dyan's alimony claim was not fully met and Grant's access to their daughter was nowhere near as restricted as she had requested.

> **Once the female has used the male for procreation, she turns on him and literally devours him.**
>
> CARY GRANT

Paradise lost? The poet Milton was only six weeks into his first marriage, to Mary Powell, when he started work on a publication in defence of divorce, *The Doctrine and Discipline of Divorce, Restored to the Good of Both Sexes*. In the seventeenth century, divorce was only granted in the case of adultery, but Milton championed the cause for divorce on the grounds of incompatibility. One source of inspiration could well have been the fact that his wife had already left him.

The first months of marriage had their own complications for another seventeenth-century poet, John Donne. In December 1601 he and Ann More married in secret, and it wasn't until the following February that they broke the news to Ann's father. He was furious, which maybe justified the original idea of marrying in secret, but the less agreeable result was that Donne was sacked from his job (his boss was Ann's uncle) and sent to prison. One letter that Donne wrote from his cell finished with the words 'John Donne, Ann Donne, Un-done.' Happily, in April, the Court of Audiences upheld the validity of their marriage and the pair were reunited.

66 **Some women pick men to marry — others pick them to pieces.**

MAE WEST

It is something of a mystery why young Mae West picked a dancer named Frank Wallace to marry. When he proposed to her, she accepted only on condition that he wouldn't tell her mother. It was, according to Ms West, a 'kissless' marriage; looking back, she claimed that she had never been in love with him and that they always slept in separate rooms. In the end she engineered their separation by putting her husband's name forward as a dancer for a forty-week tour of the States. Frank got the job and that was the last they saw of each other, until several years later when he sued for maintenance and half of her property, which by then amounted to a considerable fortune, but Mae held out and Frank didn't get a cent.

The affair between Franz Liszt and the fiery Lola Montez came to an end on the day he unveiled a statue of Beethoven in Bonn; the solemn banquet afterwards was suddenly disturbed by a gatecrashing Lola, who treated the distinguished gathering to a flamboyant dance on top of the table! In the early hours of the following morning, Liszt sneaked out of their bedroom, never to return. When Lola awoke alone and realized what had happened, she vented her anger in typical fashion by hurling various pieces of ornate furniture out of the window.

# CHAPTER FOURTEEN

# LOVE AND DEATH

*Dying words, dying deeds, duels, dual suicides and the mourning after*

If his loving wife had not talked him into going to the theatre one fateful evening in 1865, Abraham Lincoln would have escaped assassination from the gun of John Wilkes Booth, or at least postponed it. Abe was quite happy to spend the evening at home, but he finally gave in. 'All right Mary, I'll go,' he said. 'But if I don't go down in history as the Martyr President I miss my guess . . .'

> **Marriage is neither heaven nor hell, it is simply purgatory.**
>
> ABRAHAM LINCOLN

A love of sex saved Henry III from assassination in the autumn of 1239. The day started badly when a deranged poet named Ribault burst into Henry's court; claiming that *he* was the rightful King of England, he demanded the crown. He was swiftly marched away, but Henry gave orders that he should not be treated harshly as the poor man was clearly mad. That same night, Ribault, having been released in line with the King's wishes, stole into Henry's bedchamber with a dagger and hid under the bed. Then, in a sudden frenzy, he leapt out and plunged the dagger into the shape beneath the bedclothes, screaming abuse with each fresh stab. Fortunately for Henry, the wounds were suffered only by his mattress and bolster, as he was busy enjoying himself in the queen's chamber. This time Ribault was treated rather more harshly; he was executed.

Henry VIII's fifth wife, Catherine Howard, was beheaded in 1542 for her adulterous affair with Thomas Culpeper. As she stood on the scaffold, she remained defiant in her love. 'Long before the King took me, I loved Culpeper. And I wish to God I had done as he wished me; for at the time the King wanted to take me, he urged me to say that I was pledged to him . . . But sin blinded me, and greed of grandeur, and since mine is the fault, mine also is the suffering and my great sorrow is that Culpeper should have to die through me. I die a Queen but I would rather die the wife of Culpeper. Good people, I beg you, pray for me . . .'

In the third century, Saint Agatha of Sicily came to a particularly nasty end for refusing the advances of Sicily's Roman governor. Before being burnt for this 'crime', she underwent horrific torture and is usually depicted in church carvings and paintings with her breasts either held in pincers, pierced with a sword, or severed and resting on a tray before her. As the result of a rather bad painting that made her breasts look like loaves of bread, it is a custom to bless bread on her feast day, 5 February.

At his execution Charles I is known to have worn an extra shirt so that he would not shiver from the cold and have the public think he was shivering in fear. A more personal preparation in his final hour was to open a secret compartment in one of his royal medallions. Inside was a miniature portrait of his beloved Queen Henrietta, at which Charles took one last look before stepping out to face his executioner.

The artist Salvador Dali was out for a walk along the clifftops with his wife and constant inspiration Gala, when he suddenly seized her and kissed her 'carnivorously'. Holding her by the hair, he demanded that she tell him what to do with her. 'Tell it to me obscenely,' he said, 'so I can become a man and an animal.' Gala's request was simple, though not what he had been expecting. 'Kill me,' she said. Dali never forgot the surprise he felt at that moment. Nor did he forget Gala's courage. Still gripping her hair, he looked down at the crashing sea below, but then realized that Gala had driven 'the forces of death' out of him. They continued their walk and, together, lived eccentrically ever after.

> **" I'd rather see a woman die, any day, than see her happy with someone else.**
>
> PABLO PICASSO

The notion of dying for love held no appeal for one peer of the Victorian era, Lord Jersey. Lord Palmerston, later to become Prime Minister, was one of many gentleman who enjoyed the favours of Lady Jersey as a mistress, safe in the knowledge that he would never be challenged to a duel by an outraged husband. Lord Jersey had once remarked that if he started fighting duels with his wife's lovers he would find himself up against half the men in London.

In the early seventeenth century, a particularly civilized form of duel caused the loser no damage apart from wounded pride. When the Poet Laureate, Ben Jonson, was challenged to a 'rhyming duel' by a gentleman named Joshua Sylvester, it was Sylvester who fired the first shot:

> I, Sylvester
> Kissed your sister.

Jonson hit back with:

> I, Ben Jonson
> Kissed your wife.

'That doesn't rhyme!' Sylvester protested. 'No,' replied Blank Verse Ben, 'but it's true.'

The composer Puccini gave his wife Elvira many a reason to doubt his fidelity, but on one occasion her jealousy was fatally misplaced. Finding her husband chatting late at night with their servant Doria, she leapt to the conclusion that they were lovers. After hurling abuse at the two of them, she spent the rest of the night hammering on the poor girl's bedroom door. Word soon went round the village that Elvira had caught Puccini and Doria doing more than talking. 'No smoke without fire' was the general attitude, despite Doria's frantic protestations. Within weeks, worn down by the gossip and the shame she was made to feel, she took a lethal dose of poison. An autopsy revealed that she had died a virgin.

H. G. Wells found it very hard to say no, but on one of the rare occasions when he *did*, he thought he had a suicide on his hands. Having been invited by a lady to meet some friends of hers, Wells arrived at the house to find the lady all alone, dressed in a gown and nothing else. At this, her first proposition, the word 'no' characteristically failed to fall from his lips. As he recounted in his memoirs, '"This must end," said I, "this must end," – allowing myself to be dragged upstairs.' They met intermittently after that but when he decided the affair *had* to end, he gave his maid instructions not to let the woman into his house. One night, though, when the usual maid was out, Wells wandered into his study to find his lady-friend lying seductively on the carpet in her unbuttoned mackintosh and (again) not much else. For once Wells controlled himself and went to call the porter. They returned to find her lying on a blood-spattered carpet, her wrists slashed with a razor. As it happened, this was an old trick of hers – she had learnt how to draw a spectacular amount of blood without causing lasting damage. Still, Wells had to pull a lot of strings to keep the newspapers from printing the story. Many years later they met again, but she was now quite happily married; this time Wells and the lady's wrists escaped unscathed.

There was a lot of blood when Mark Antony, facing defeat by the army of Octavian, decided to do the noble thing and run onto his sword. Unfortunately, not having had much practice, he failed to score a direct hit; his death was therefore painfully long in coming. The only consolation for such a bungled suicide was that he was still alive when he was carried to Cleopatra – he died in his lover's arms. Cleopatra soon followed him. Octavian wanted her kept alive, but she had a deadly cobra smuggled to her room in a basket of figs. Having left a request that she be buried beside Antony, she held the snake to her flesh and despatched herself with a touch more style (and a lot less mess) than Antony had managed.

After the dual suicide of Adolf Hitler and Eva Braun, the bodies were soaked in petrol and set alight, in accordance with Hitler's last request. This was a precaution against the corpses meeting the same fate as those of Benito Mussolini and his mistress Clara Petacci. They had been shot by Italian partisans two days earlier and the bodies had then been put on display for public ridicule, hung upside down from the rafters of a Milan petrol station. Some 'sightseers' even fired more bullets into the corpses, in revenge for loved ones who had died at the hands of the fascists.

Nancy Spungen, girlfriend of the Sex Pistols' bassist, Sid Vicious, either killed herself or was killed by Sid when both were drunk and drugged up to the eyeballs. 'Nancy was great,' said Sid, 'because she and I were the same – we both hated everyone.' Sid died from a massive heroin overdose whilst on bail, facing trial for Nancy's murder.

Louis Armstrong, who died from kidney failure in July 1971, was followed within a month by his second wife Lil. Having never remarried since their separation forty years previously, Lil was playing the piano at a memorial concert for Louis in Chicago, when she suddenly collapsed at the keyboard and died.

Death mid-act also came to Attila the Hun, on his wedding night in 453 AD. The lusty warrior had married several other wives, so it wasn't the novelty of the experience that killed him, just the excitement.

It was whilst making love to a married woman that Pope Leo VIII met his maker. The fatal blow was not struck by a furious husband but someone rather more powerful. At his moment of ecstasy, the Pope suffered an attack of paralysis from which he never recovered. God had seen enough.

> **My heart cannot be happy even for an hour without love.**
>
> CATHERINE THE GREAT

A handful of royal figures have met their ends whilst out riding a horse, but Catherine the Great of Russia must be the only one to have come to grief whilst being ridden by one.

Love and death were inextricably linked for Mary Shelley, the author of *Frankenstein*, when she declared her undying love for the poet Percy Bysshe Shelley whilst the pair stood by her mother's grave at Old Saint Pancras Church. Her father, who was far from happy about the relationship, accused Shelley of seducing his daughter on her mother's grave. This story was refuted by her half-sister Jane, who had accompanied them on their graveyard stroll, and who then played the role of gooseberry way beyond the call of duty by joining them in their elopement to France.

Samuel Pepys gave himself a macabre birthday treat when he went along to Westminster Abbey to see the body of a dead queen. Queen Katherine, wife of Henry V, had been buried for three hundred years, when her coffin was disturbed during building work on the chapel. Pepys was amongst those who went for a peek at her embalmed corpse and, naturally, he recorded the event in his diary: 'Here we did see, by particular favour, the body of Queen Katharine of Valois . . .' But *seeing* her wasn't enough. '. . . and I had the upper part of her body in my hands . . .' But *holding* her wasn't enough. '. . . and I did kiss her mouth, reflecting upon it that I did kiss a queen, and that this was my birthday, thirty-six years old, that I did kiss a queen.' That is as far as the diary entry goes, and, hopefully, as far as Pepys went too.

The last wish of Henry VIII, not the greatest PR-man marriage has ever known, was to be buried beside Jane Seymour. She was the only of his wives to have left him against his will, although she had to die (in childbirth) to do it. The remains of the poet John Milton lie in the church of St Giles, Cripplegate. Although he survived three wives, it was a fair reflection of his views on women and marriage that he should request to be buried next to his father.

66 **The worst of having a romance of any kind is that it leaves one so unromantic.**
OSCAR WILDE

Shah Jehan was laid to rest beside the body of his wife Mumtaz Mahal, in the world's most expensive and most beautiful mausoleum. After Mumtaz's death in 1639, the Taj Mahal took 20,000 men twenty years to build. A more modest funeral was the one of Mahatma Gandhi's wife, Kasturbai, whose last request was that she be cremated in a sari made from yarn which Gandhi himself had spun.

On her deathbed, Queen Caroline told George II that he should marry again after she was gone. 'No,' George replied, 'I shall have mistresses.' Caroline couldn't see what that had to do with it; marriage had never stopped him having mistresses before. In the twenty-three years that he lived after her death, George did not marry but, true to his word, enjoyed his share of mistresses. In 1760 he died on the throne, suffering a stroke whilst sitting on the lavatory. In Westminster Abbey he was reunited with his wife – Caroline's coffin had been fitted with a special sliding panel so that George's body could be laid to rest beside hers.

Another monarch fond of mistresses was Edward VII. When he died in 1910, his wife Queen Alexandra kept vigil over his body in Buckingham Palace. Eying the coffin across the dimly lit room, she couldn't help remarking to her lady-in-waiting that this was the first night in ages that she had known exactly where he was.

'Kiss me, Hardy' are the most famous words that Lord Nelson uttered shortly before his death at Trafalgar, but they were not his last. After Hardy had complied with his admiral's request, Nelson spoke to the ship's chaplain. 'I have *not* been a *great* sinner,' he told him. Then, through the agony of his dying moments, he begged the chaplain to ensure that his mistress, Lady Hamilton, would be well provided for. Nelson had left in his will a request that Lady Hamilton and the daughter she had borne him be cared for by a grateful nation. However, the nation elected to care for Nelson's wife Fanny instead. Nine years after Trafalgar, Lady Hamilton died penniless in Calais.

King Charles II showed similar concern for his mistress, Nell Gwynne, in his dying words, 'Let not poor Nelly starve', and another Charlie whose last thoughts were for a lady other than his wife was Charles Dickens, who called for the actress Ellen Ternan. Queen Victoria was more loyal to her spouse, even though Albert had been dead for forty years. 'Oh, that peace may come, Bertie!' she cried, before rejoining him in the hereafter. So ended four decades of personal mourning, during which she had always dressed in black and, each night, gone to bed clutching his nightshirt, with his picture on the pillow beside her. At her insistence, memorials to Albert had been erected all over the country – not that Albert had been the sort to approve of such aggrandisement. She refused to appear in public for two full years after his death, and when she finally did it was to unveil a statue of Bertie. It was only after Albert had been dead for eight years that the staff at Windsor Castle were allowed to take off their black armbands.

The prostitutes of Paris wore black scarves, not round their arms but over their 'private' parts, out of respect for one of their most illustrious clients, Victor Hugo. The author of *The Hunchback of Notre Dame* can have had no back problems himself – he spent so much time in brothels, the wonder is that he found the time (and energy) to write. When he died, the city's prostitutes were given a unique grant by the Government, so that they could knock off from work on the day of his funeral without suffering a loss of income.

> **66 Life is a flower of which love is the honey.**
>
> VICTOR HUGO

At the funeral of his first wife, in 1908, Stalin watched the coffin being lowered into its grave and grasped the hand of his old schoolfriend, Iremashvili. 'This creature used to soften my stony heart,' he whispered. 'When she died, all my warm feeling for people died with her.' It was after her death that Joseph Djugashvili started using the name Stalin, the Russian word *stal* giving him a name with a heart of *steel*.

Richard Wagner's wife Cosima was so distraught at her husband's death that she fell down and clung on to his corpse for a whole day and night. Before his funeral, at which a full orchestra played the Siegfried Funeral March from Wagner's own *Götterdämmerung*, Cosima placed a lock of her hair in his coffin, on his heart.

Dante Gabriel Rossetti rested a book of his own poems, handwritten and unpublished, in the coffin of his wife Elizabeth. As so much of his work owed its inspiration to the woman he had loved, it seemed only fitting that some should be buried with her. However, as the years passed, Rossetti could not help thinking of those poems which lay in her grave, some of his finest work, unpublished and unread. In the end he was granted a licence by the Home Secretary to dig up the coffin and remove the book. The collection was finally published as *Poems* in 1870, seven years after their burial.

## IN MEMORIAM

It has been claimed that Rasputin's reputation as 'Russia's Greatest Love-Machine' owed much to a wart on his penis, which provided added stimulation. This has never been proven, but the evidence may still be around if the legend is true that his penis was chopped off from the rest of his dead body and kept in a velvet purse by a group of elderly ladies with fond memories. Quite what they did with this shrivelled momento is anyone's guess, but it can have been no less useful than the souvenir Sir Walter Raleigh's wife kept of her husband. For the thirty years from Sir Walter's execution to her own death, she kept his head in a red velvet bag.

# IN THE NAME OF LOVE . . .

## A Quick Quiz

1   Frank Sinatra liked to call his young wife, Mia Farrow, 'doll face'. She called *him* after a popular cartoon character. Which one?

    A. Popeye     B. Charlie Brown     C. Goofy

2   Which British radio DJ calls his wife 'The Pig'?

    A. John Peel     B. Jimmy Saville
    C. Dave Lee Travis

3   Which British Prime Minister was known to his wife as 'Pug'?

    A. Benjamin Disraeli     B. David Lloyd George
    C. Winston Churchill

4   Which famous German's penis was called *Herr Schönfuss* (Mr Fine-foot) by his wife?

    A. Richard Wagner     B. Johann Wolfgang Goethe
    C. Immanuel Kant

5    Which famous American couple call each other 'Daddy' and 'Mommy'?

   A. George and Barbara Bush
   B. Gerald and Betty Ford
   C. Ronald and Nancy Reagan

6    Which English poet affectionately called his wife 'Ugly', 'Filth' and 'Beastliness'?

   A. T. S. Eliot      B. Robert Graves
   C. John Betjeman

7    Which great thinker called his wife 'Princess' after the princess in a fairy story, from whose lips fell roses and pearls?

   A. Sigmund Freud      B. Albert Einstein
   C. Karl Marx

8    What was Richard Burton's favourite name for Elizabeth Taylor?

   A. Miss Tits      B. Fred      C. Ocean

9    One of the statesmen at the Yalta conference in 1945 once referred to intellectual women as 'herrings with ideas'. Who was it?

   A. Churchill      B. Roosevelt      C. Stalin

10   George Formby had two houses called Beryldene, a cruiser called Lady Beryl, a motor launch called Crazy Beryl, and a dinghy called Baby Beryl. What was his wife called?

   A. Beryl      B. Beryl      C. Beryl

# IN THE NAME OF LOVE – QUIZ ANSWERS

1  B. Charlie Brown.

2  A. John Peel – because of the way she snorts when she laughs.

3  C. Winston Churchill – he called her 'Pussy-Kat'.

4  B. Johann Wolfgang Goethe.

5  C. Ronald and Nancy Reagan.

6  C. John Betjeman – in return, she called him 'Dung' and 'Poofy' (because of his puff-ball hair).

7  A. Sigmund Freud.

8  C. 'Ocean'. He called her 'Miss Tits', 'Fred' and more besides, but 'Ocean' was the most affectionate, because she was 'boundless'.

9  C. Stalin.

10  Correct.

# LOVE'S PURSUIT

## – Trivia Quiz

1   When Elizabeth II and Prince Philip were courting, which musical number was 'their tune'?

   A. 'A Fine Romance'      B. 'Cheek to Cheek'
   C. 'People Will Say We're in Love'

2   Which great opera star was arrested in the zoo of New York's Central Park and subsequently convicted of pinching a woman's bottom?

   A. Enrico Caruso      B. Luciano Pavarotti
   C. Placido Domingo

3   How old was Myra Brown when she married her third cousin, Jerry Lee Lewis in 1958?

   A. 11      B. 13      C. 15

4   With regard to his lovemaking, which US President has been called 'as compulsive as Mussolini – up against the wall, Signora, if you have five minutes'?

   A. J. F. Kennedy  B. F. D. Roosevelt  C. Richard Nixon

5    Which one of these men did Lucretia Borgia *not* sleep
     with?

     A. Her father      B. Leonardo da Vinci
     C. The Pope

6    Which Roman emperor kicked his pregnant second wife
     to death for nagging him?

     A. Caligula      B. Nero      C. Claudius

7    After Marilyn Monroe's death, a signed photograph
     was found, bearing the inscription 'to Marilyn, with
     love and thanks'. Who was it from?

     A. Bobby Kennedy      B. Arthur Miller
     C. Albert Einstein

8    The 'It' Girl, '20s film star Clara Bow, was said by her
     secretary to have slept with the entire football team of
     the University of California. The line-up included a
     certain Marion Morrison. By what name did Marion
     later become better known?

     A. Gary Cooper      B. John Wayne      C. Errol Flynn

9    Who was so 'violently in love' with Lillie Langtry that
     he slept overnight on her doorstep?

     A. Edward Langtry      B. Edward VII
     C. Oscar Wilde

10   How many wives is 'wise' King Solomon reputed to
     have had?

     A. None      B. 7      C. 700

## LOVE'S PURSUIT – QUIZ ANSWERS

1    C.   'People Will Say We're in Love' – from the musical *Oklahoma*, which the young couple saw on one of their first nights out together. Princess Elizabeth's copy of the record was soon worn down through repeated playings.

2    A. Enrico Caruso.

3    B. 13. Jerry Lee Lewis had to abandon his tour of England due to booing and jeering from audiences who put more conservative limits on a man's freedom to rock'n'roll.

4    A. J. F. Kennedy – according to a lady who shared a room with one of his many conquests.

5    B. Leonardo da Vinci. The fact that Pope Alexander VI and her father were one and the same person should take nothing away from Lucretia's remarkable achievement.

6    B. Nero.

7    C. Albert Einstein.

8    B. John Wayne.

9    C. Oscar Wilde.

10    C. 700. In case he ever felt lonely, he also kept 300 concubines.

# BIBLIOGRAPHY

Ackroyd, Peter; *T. S. Eliot* (Hamish Hamilton, 1984)

Adams, Leon; *Larry Hagman: A Biography* (Star Books, 1988)

Allen, Woody; *Four films of Woody Allen* (Random House, 1982)

Allen, Woody; *Without Feathers* (Sphere, 1978)

Anger, Kenneth; *Hollywood Babylon* (Arrow Books, 1986)

Anger, Kenneth; *Hollywood Babylon II* (Arrow Books, 1986)

Bacall, Lauren; *By Myself* (Coronet/Hodder & Stoughton, 1980)

Balogh, Penelope; *Freud: A Biographical Introduction* (Studio Vista)

Bell, Simon, Curtis, Richard and Fielding, Helen: *Who's Had Who: In Association with Berk's Rogerage* (Faber & Faber, 1987)

Bhutto, Benazir; *Daughter of the East: An Autobiography* (Hamish Hamilton, 1989)

Blundell, Nigel, edited by; *The World's Greatest Scandals of the 20th Century* (Octopus, 1986)

Botham, Kathy; *Living With a Legend* (Grafton Books, 1987)

Boulay, Shirley du; *Tutu: Voice of the Voiceless* (Hodder & Stoughton, 1988)

Bourne, Peter; *Castro* (Macmillan, 1987)

Bragg, Melvyn; *Rich: The Life of Richard Burton* (Hodder & Stoughton, 1988)

Brayfield, Celia; *Glitter: The Truth about Fame* (Chatto & Windus, 1985)

Brent, Peter; *Charles Darwin* (William Heinemann, 1981)

Bret, David; *The Piaf Legend* (Robson Books, 1988)

Brown, Michele and O'Connor, Ann; *Hammer and Tongues* (Dent, 1986)

# BIBLIOGRAPHY

Browne, Jennifer; *The Prime Ministers: Stories and Anecdotes from Number 10* (W. H. Allen, 1987)

Bruccoli, Matthew J.; *Some Sort of Epic Grandeur: The Life of F. Scott Fitzgerald* (Hodder & Stoughton, 1981)

Bryan III, J. and Murphy, Charles J. V.; *The Windsor Story* (Granada, 1979)

Bullock, Alan; *Hitler: A Study in Tyranny* (Penguin, 1969)

Bushell, Peter; *London's Secret History* (Constable & Co., 1983)

Cabanne, Pierre; *Van Gogh* (Thames & Hudson, 1969)

Canning, John, edited by; *One Hundred Great Lives* (Souvenir, 1975)

Carr, Francis; *Mozart & Constanze* (John Murray, 1983)

Cashin, Fergus; *Mae West* (W. H. Allen, 1981)

Clark, Ronald W.; *Lenin: The Man Behind the Mask* (Faber & Faber, 1988)

Clinch, Minty; *Harrison Ford* (New English Library, 1987)

Colin, Sid; *Ella: The Life and Times of Ella Fitzgerald* (Elm Tree Books/Hamish Hamilton, 1986)

Collier, James Lincoln; *Louis Armstrong: A Biography* (Pan, 1984)

Collier, Peter and Horowitz, David; *The Kennedys: An American Drama* (Pan, 1985)

Consodine, Shaun; *Barbara Streisand: The Woman, the Myth, the Music* (Century Hutchinson, 1986)

Cooper, Cary L. and Thompson, Linda; *Public Faces, Private Lives* (Fontana, 1984)

Crick, Bernard; *George Orwell: A Life* (Penguin, 1982)

Crisp, Quentin; *The Naked Civil Servant* (Fontana, 1985)

Cross, Colin; *(The Observer) Sayings of the Seventies* (David & Charles, 1979)

Domingo, Placido; *My First Forty Years* (Papermac, 1984)

Drower, G. M. F.; *Neil Kinnock: The Path to Leadership* (Weidenfeld & Nicolson, 1984)

Dunn, Clive; *Permission to Speak: An Autobiography* (Century Hutchinson, 1986)

Edwards, Anne; *Katherine Hepburn: A Biography* (Hodder & Stoughton, 1986)

Feely, Terence; *Number 10: The Private Lives of Six Ministers* (Sidgwick & Jackson, 1986)

Fingleton, David; *Kiri: A Biography of Kiri Te Kanawa* (Collins, 1984)

Fischer, Hans Conrad and Kock, Erich; *Ludwig van Beethoven* (Macmillan, 1983)

Fisher, Graham and Heather; *Consort: The Life and Times of Prince Philip* (W. H. Allen, 1980)

Fraser, Antonia; *Boadicea's Chariot* (Weidenfeld & Nicolson, 1988)

Fraser, Flora; *Beloved Emma: The Life of Emma, Lady Hamilton* (Weidenfeld & Nicolson, 1986)

Gartenberg, Egon; *Mahler: The Man and His Music* (Panther Books, 1987)

Goldman, Albert; *Elvis* (Macdonald, 1980)

Graham, Sheilah; *Scratch An Actor: Confessions of a Hollywood Gossip Columnist* (W. H. Allen, 1969)

Gray, Michael and Bauldie John; *All Across the Telegraph: A Bob Dylan Handbook* (Sidgwick & Jackson, 1987)

Guinness, Alec; *Blessings in Disguise* (Hamish Hamilton, 1985)

Hall, William; *Raising Caine* (Sidgwick & Jackson, 1981)

Harris, Kenneth; *David Owen: Personally Speaking* (Pan Books, 1988)

Haskins, James; *Nat King Cole: The Man and His Music* (Robson Books, 1986)

Healey, Edna; *Wives of Fame* (Sidgwick & Jackson, 1986)

Heller, Erich; *Kafka* (Fontana/Collins, 1974)

Hill, Christopher; *God's Englishman: Oliver Cromwell and the English Revolution* (Penguin, 1972)

Hillier, Bevis; *Young Betjeman* (John Murray, 1988)

Holmes, Richard; *Shelley: The Pursuit* (Weidenfeld & Nicolson, 1974)

Holroyd, Michael; *Bernard Shaw: 1, The Search for Love* (Chatto & Windus, 1988)

Hopkins, Jerry; *Bowie* (Elm Tree Books/Hamish Hamilton, 1985)

Hopkins, John; *Nick Faldo: In Perspective* (George Allen & Unwin, 1985)

Howard, Elizabeth Jane, edited by; *The Lover's Companion* (David & Charles, 1978)

Hudson, Derek; *Lewis Carroll* (Constable & Co., 1976)

# BIBLIOGRAPHY

Hudson, Rock and Davidson, Sara; *Rock Hudson: His Story* (Weidenfeld & Nicolson, 1986)

Huffington, Arianna Stassinopoulos; *Picasso: Creator & Destroyer* (Weidenfeld & Nicolson, 1988)

Jackson, Stanley; *Monsieur Butterfly: the Story of Puccini* (W. H. Allen, 1974)

Jameson, Derek; *Touched by Angels* (Ebury Press, 1988)

Jenner, Heather; *Royal Wives* (Duckworth, 1967)

Johnson, Edgar; *Charles Dickens: His Tragedy and Triumph* (Penguin, 1986)

Jones, Graham and Lynne; *I Love Sex, I Hate Sex* (New English Library/Hodder & Stoughton, 1989)

Jonge, Alex de; *Stalin and the Shaping of the Soviet Union* (Fontana, 1987)

Jonge, Alex de; *The Life and Times of Grigorii Rasputin* (Fontana/Collins, 1983)

Julian, Philippe; *Oscar Wilde* (Paladin, 1971)

Keays, Sara; *A Question of Judgment* (Quintessential Press, 1985)

Kelley, Kitty; *His Way* (Bantam, 1987)

Kinnell, Peter; *More Erotic Failures* (Futura, 1985)

Knightley, Philip and Kennedy, Caroline; *An Affair of State (The Profumo Case and the Framing of Stephen Ward)* (Jonathan Cape, 1987)

Latham, Robert; *The Shorter Pepys* (Bell & Hyman, 1985)

Lawrence, Frieda; *Not I, but the Wind* (Heinemann/Granada, 1983)

Lerner, Laurence; *Love and Marriage: Literature and its Social Context* (Edward Arnold, 1979)

Lesley, Cole; *The Life of Noël Coward* (Jonathan Cape, 1976)

Levi, Peter; *The Life and Times of William Shakespeare* (Macmillan, 1988)

Longford, Elizabeth; *Eminent Victorian Women* (Weidenfeld & Nicolson, 1981)

Longford, Elizabeth; *Winston Churchill* (Sidgwick & Jackson, 1974)

Lulu; *Lulu: Her Autobiography* (Granada, 1985)

Mandela, Winnie; *Part of My Soul* (Penguin, 1985)

Mansell, Nigel and Allsop, Derek; *Driven to Win* (Stanley Paul/Century Hutchinson, 1988)

Masters, Brian; *The Swinging Sixties* (Constable & Co., 1985)

McIntosh, William Currie and Weaver, William; *The Private Cary Grant* (Sidgwick & Jackson, 1987)

Miles, Rosalind, compiled by; *Modest Proposals* (Macdonald & Co., 1984)

Morgan, Janet; *Agatha Christie: A Biography* (Collins, 1984)

Morgan, Ted; *FDR: A Biography* (Grafton Books, 1986)

Moseley, Roy; *Roger Moore: A Biography* (New English Library, 1985)

Mosley, Leonard; *The Real Walt Disney: A Biography* (Grafton Books/Collins, 1986)

Murray, Patricia; *Margaret Thatcher: A Profile* (W. H. Allen, 1980)

Nanda, B. R.; *Mahatma Gandhi: A Biography* (Oxford University Press, 1982)

Navratilova, Martina with Vecsey, George; *Being Myself* (William Collins Sons & Co., 1985)

Neale, J. E.; *Queen Elizabeth I* (Penguin, 1988)

Nicholas, Margaret, edited by; *The World's Greatest Lovers* (Octopus, 1985)

Nicholas, Margaret, edited by; *The World's Wickedest Women* (Octopus, 1984)

Orga, Ates; *Chopin: His Life and Times* (Midas Books, 1983)

Pearson, Hesketh; *Conan Doyle* (Unwin Hyman, 1987)

Porter, Janet Street; *Scandal* (Allen Lane/Penguin, 1981)

Presley, Priscilla Beaulieu; *Elvis and Me* (Century Hutchinson, 1985)

Randall, David; *Royal Follies: A Chronicle of Royal Misbehaviour* (W. H. Allen, 1987)

Rivers, Joan with Meryman, Richard; *Enter Talking* (W. H. Allen, 1987)

Rix, Brian; *My Farce from my Elbow* (Secker & Warburg, 1975)

Robyns, Gwen; *Barbara Cartland: An Authorised Biography* (Sidgwick & Jackson, 1984)

Rowse, A. L.; *Milton: the Puritan: Portrait of a Mind* (Macmillan, 1986)

Salewicz, Chris; *McCartney: The Biography* (Macdonald & Co., 1986)

Scarisbrick, J. J.; *Henry VIII* (Eyre Methuen, 1976)

# BIBLIOGRAPHY

Schofield, Carey; *Jagger* (Methuen, 1983)

Scudamore, Pauline; *Spike Milligan: A Biography* (Granada/Grafton, 1985)

Secrest, Meryle; *Salvador Dali: The Surrealist Jester* (Grafton, 1988)

Smith, Gus; *Wogan* (Star, 1988)

Spink, Reginald; *Hans Christian Andersen and His World* (Thames & Hudson)

Stoney, Barbara; *Enid Blyton: A Biography* (Hodder & Stoughton, 1986)

Summers, Anthony; *Goddess: the Secret Lives of Marilyn Monroe* (Victor Gollancz, 1985)

Tabori, Paul; *A Pictorial History of Love* (Spring Books)

Taylor, Ronald; *Franz Liszt: The Man and the Musician* (Grafton, 1986)

Thomas, Bob; *Astaire: The Man, the Dancer* (Weidenfeld & Nicolson, 1985)

Thomas, Bob; *Liberace: The Untold Story* (Weidenfeld & Nicolson, 1988)

Walker, Alexander; *Peter Sellers* (Coronet/Hodder & Stoughton, 1982)

Walton, Ashley and Fincher, Jayne; *Charles & Diana: The First Five Years* (Scott Publishing Co., 1986)

Weiner, Jon; *Come Together: John Lennon in His Time* (Faber & Faber, 1985)

Welfare, Simon; *Great Honeymoon Disasters* (Arthur Barker/Weidenfeld, 1986)

Wilson, Colin and Seaman, Donald; *Scandal!* (Weidenfeld & Nicolson, 1986)

Wilson, Dick; *Mao: The People's Emperor* (Futura, 1980)

Wilson, Joan; *A Soldier's Wife: Wellington's Marriage* (Weidenfeld & Nicolson, 1987)

Grateful acknowledgement is made for permission to quote from the following:

*Agatha Christie: A biography* by Janet Morgan, William Collins Sons & Co Ltd

*An Affair of State* by Phillip Knightley and Caroline Kennedy, Jonathan Cape Ltd

*Barbra Streisand: The woman, the myth, the music* by Shaun Considine, Random Century Group Ltd

*Being Myself* by Martina Navratilova with George Vecsey, William Collins Sons & Co Ltd

*By Myself* by Lauren Bacall, Jonathan Cape Ltd

*Castro* by Peter Bourne, Macmillan Publishing Ltd

*Conan Doyle* by Hesketh Pearson, Unwin Hyman Ltd

*Elvis and Me* by Priscilla Beaulieu Presley, Random Century Ltd

*Enid Blyton: A biography* by Barbara Stoney, Hodder & Stoughton Ltd

*Freud: A biographical introduction* by Penelope Balogh, Charles Scribner's Sons and Macmillan Publishing Company

*George Orwell: A life* by Bernard Crick, A. M. Heath Ltd

*I Love Sex I Hate Sex* by Graham and Lynne Jones, New English Library

'In a Bath Teashop', © The John Betjeman Estate

'I Wish I Were in Love Again' Rodgers and Hart, © Chappell & Co Ltd

*Kafka* by Erich Heller, William Collins Sons & Co Ltd

*Katharine Hepburn: A biography* by Anne Edwards, Hodder & Stoughton Ltd

*Louis Armstrong: A biography* by James Lincoln Collier, Michael Joseph Ltd

*Ludwig van Beethoven* by Hans Conrad Fischer & Erich Koch, Macmillan Publishers Ltd

*Modest Proposals* by Rosalind Miles, MacDonald Ltd

*More Erotic Failures* by Peter Kinnell, MacDonald Ltd

*Nat King Cole: The man and his music* by James Haskins, Robson Books Ltd

*Not I, but the Wind* by Frieda Lawrence, William Heinemann Ltd

*Permission To Speak: An autobiography* by Clive Dunn, Anthony Sheil Associates Ltd

*Public Faces Private Lives* by C. L. Cooper and L. Thompson, William Collins Sons & Co Ltd

*Rich: The life of Richard Burton* by Melvyn Bragg, Hodder & Stoughton Ltd

*Roger Moore: A biography* by Roy Moseley, New English Library

*Stalin and the Shaping of the Soviet Union* by Alex de Jonge, William Collins Sons & Co Ltd

*The Kennedys: An American dream* by Peter Collier and David Horowitz, William Heinemann Ltd

*The Life of Noel Coward* by Cole Lesley, Jonathan Cape Ltd

*The Private Cary Grant* by William Currie McIntosh and William Weaver, Sidgwick & Jackson Ltd

*The Private Lives of Six Ministers* by Terence Feely, Sidgwick & Jackson Ltd

*The Search for Love* by Michael Holroyd, Jonathan Cape Ltd

*The Swinging Sixties* by Brian Masters, Constable & Co Ltd

*The Truth About Fame* by Celia Brayfield, Chatto Windus Ltd

*The World's Greatest Lovers* edited by Margaret Nicholas, Paul Hamlyn Publishing

*Wives of Fame* by Edna Healey, Sidgwick & Jackson Ltd

*Young Betjeman* by Bevis Hillier, John Murray Ltd

Every effort has been made to locate holders of copyright material used in this book and the publisher will be happy to acknowledge in future editions anyone who has been omitted.